MEMOIRS OF A PARACHUTE INFANTRYMAN

THE MIGHTY TIGER

SGT. ROBERT J. BRODERICK

SHINE-A-LIGHT
PRESS

Visit Shine-A-Light Press on our website: www.ShineALightPress.
com;

> on Twitter: @SALPress;
> and on Instagram: @ShineALightCorp

The Shine-A-Light Press logo is a trademark of Shine-A-Light Corp.

The Mighty Tiger: Memoirs of a Parachute Infantryman
Copyright © 2022 by Robert T. Broderick

Edited by Chris and Andrea Elston. Book layout and design by Chris
Elston. Cover design by Liana Moisescu

Library of Congress Control Number: 2022938972

ISBN: 978-1-953158-86-4

For my darling wife and our wonderful children, grandchildren, and great grandchildren.

ACKNOWLEDGMENTS

Much of the memorabilia that I had accumulated during the war years would have continued to languish at the bottom of some desk drawer had it not been for the gentle, if not persistent plodding of my wife and daughters. They had insisted I could put together the bits and pieces to come up with a history of my life in uniform. Considering that it all happened over a half century ago, I had grave doubts as to the prospects for success.

I can't remember when I started this, but as the months slipped by, I often said to hell with it and just gave up. But my lovely ladies would have none of that, so I struggled forward.

It was my big girl, Carol, who kept the project alive. She had repeatedly put up with my mental lapses, disjointed and repetitious paragraphs, countless mistakes and more re-writes than can be imagined. Without her, this brief narrative would not have happened.

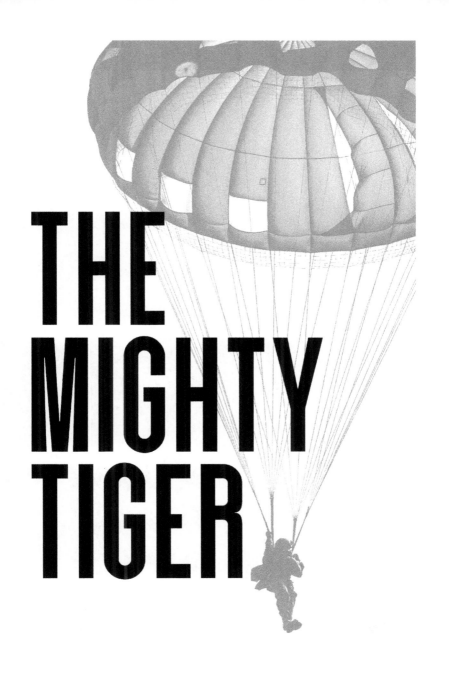

THE
MIGHTY
TIGER

You probably will find my "memoirs" interesting even though they are purely subjective and written with my children and grand children in mind: No blood an guts, booze nor ladies. And I have skipped hilari. sometime macabre, possibly illegal, immoral and other details of life in the Paratroops that helped u retain our sanity. That stuff is best left for th reunions wherein we can lie to each other with impunity.

Memory being what it is, I make no claim as to historical accuracy nor factual accounting of what m or may not have transpired during those long month But in many ways the photos, letters and other memorabilia that I had stored away long ago – when memories of events were still fresh – have help put most of the pieces together.

When my eldest granddaughter was about ten ye old she sat down at her grandmother's typewriter a pecked out a brief synopsis of life as she viewed it. Among other things, her grandmother was the "g fairy godmother" and I was the "King, the mity tig Needless to say the family picked up on that "mity tiger" and over time I became the "Mighty Tiger" & my wife, children and grandchildren. Hence the title of my brief memoirs.

War is a country no traveler ever forgets. It haunts those who survive the journey as no other experience. The memories of war cling to the mind with astonishing tenacity, and sometimes, in the dark of night when the glow of your cigarette is a distant fire in some place most people have never heard of, nothing seems to equal their demand for attention.

Author unknown

1

Somehow fate seems to lie in wait for the unwary. How could I have possibly known that the infantry was in my future and would forever cast its shadow over my life?

The evening of December 11, 1939, Dick Gaston came into the local drug store at the corner of 45th and Latona where Stan Bever was playing the store's only pinball machine as Bill Parfitt and I watched. Dick was a corporal in Headquarters Battery, 2nd Battalion, 146th Field Artillery, Washington National Guard. His uniform was the standard WWI type artilleryman's "boots and britches," and we decided, as a laugh, to go down to the new armory and watch Dick "march."

I don't know who decided we ought to enlist, but enlist we did. Actually, upon further reflection, it must have been Stan as he was the first to do it. Oddly, both Bill and I had been talking about joining the Naval Air Reserve at Sand Point, but at the time I was not quite old enough. As it was, I had to lie about my age to join the Guards. And so, the three of us, Stan, Bill and I – the three Musketeers – lightly entered into something that was to profoundly affect our lives.

When I told my father what I had done, he just wondered aloud if it had been the right thing to do, but recognized that my brother, John, was already in the Naval Reserve, and Tom was in the ROTC at the University of Washington and would soon transfer to the 205th Coast Artillery, Washington National Guard, as a sergeant.

Initially, we were issued uniforms of WWI vintage: coarse wool, whatever sizes were available. But just before summer camp at Camp Murray, located adjacent to Army and Air Force Joint Base Lewis-McChord, we were issued regulation OD's, and the boots, britches, and heavy woolens were gone forever.

With the war in Europe in progress, our drill nights went from once a week to twice a week. As a private, I received one dollar a drill night. So now I was making two dollars a week. Not bad – a small but welcome addition to my empty pocketbook in the very tough job market of 1940.

That summer saw us at Camp Murray for participation in Army maneuvers. I was a message center clerk. The regular Army men considered us Boy Scouts and paid but passing contempt for us. But, at our level, it made little difference, and all of us enjoyed Army life in the field. But I do remember one evening, as an infantry outfit from Montana came through our area on a "forced" march, sweating, cursing, and stumbling along, burdened with rifles and heavy packs and all the other paraphernalia of the foot soldier. We thought they were nuts. Somehow fate seems to lie in wait for the unwary. How could I possibly have known that the infantry was in my future and would forever cast its shadow over my life?

On the 16th of September in 1940, the Guard was inducted into Federal Service for a year of active duty. For Stan and Bill it was to be five long years of active service including forty-one months in the South Pacific. For me, it was just nine days. I was given a medical discharge because of malfunctioning kidneys.

It is hard for me, even after all these years, to describe the utter personal devastation of suddenly finding myself on the outside, cut off from my life-long buddies because of something I neither understood, nor was prepared for. Especially since a civilian doctor, who was a prominent kidney specialist in Seattle, could find nothing fundamentally wrong.

Pvt. Bob Broderick
146th Field Artillery
Washington National Guard
1940

2

I was still working swing shift when the Japanese bombed Pearl Harbor. The radio had announced the raid as we were eating breakfast that fateful Sunday morning.

On January 2, 1941, I went to work for the Boeing Airplane Company, earning a hundred dollars per month. My first job was working on various sub-assembly parts being put together at the old Kenworth Truck plant located a few blocks south of Boeing Plant #2. It was a stupefying job. All day long I put rivets in holes, handed the parts to the riveter who sat at a stationary rivet machine and foot-actuated the smashing of each rivet – one at a time - all day long. I only stayed at that job for less than a month as I was then transferred to Plant #1 (the original Red Barn) where working on the huge 314 Clippers, I spent a very pleasant spring and summer.

On most weekends, Stan and Bill had the usual passes,

and we continued to fool around much as before. In fact, they seldom even wore their uniforms. But in August, I was transferred back to Plant #2 and put on the swing shift, so I began to see less and less of the guys. Initially, I worked in the balcony paint shop doping B-17 control surfaces that, in those days, were fabric-covered. It was another boring job. After a couple months of smelling dope (aka lacquer,) I asked to be transferred down to the main floor to begin work on the second B-17E to be built. When I arrived, that huge assembly area was empty except for a B-17E that was largely completed, and the skeleton of the second one that I began working on. Both of these airplanes were assembled largely from blueprints and the guidance of the engineers and veterans of earlier model B-17 production. I was to stay on that job for the next fifteen months to be a participant and witness to the fantastic growth from that modest beginning to the mass production of such a magnificent airplane which formed the basis for America's heavy bombardment fleet.

I was still working swing shift when the Japanese bombed Pearl Harbor. The radio had announced the raid as we were eating breakfast that fateful Sunday morning. My mother had cried as my brother John was thought to be there.

A day or two later I was sent down to the neighborhood Japanese-owned dry cleaner and shoemaker to pick up some items. The entire family at the cleaners were just sobbing. The little Japanese shoemaker, who had repaired our shoes for as long as I could remember, and who had sons and daughters in

Seattle high schools, simply sat as though his world had crashed around him, as indeed it had. Both were put out of business within days.

I should mention that Bill Parfitt and I had, for many years, gone out to dinner and a movie on our respective birthdays. And as Bill's birthday is December 7th, we did not let a little war interfere with tradition. I don't remember where we had dinner, but I do know we attended some movie at the Orpheum Theater and the management kept flashing on the screen, "All military personnel report to your unit at once." Bill, in civilian clothes, simply ignored the notice.

I remember coming home from work the next night through downtown Seattle along 4th Avenue, crowds of people milling around, throwing rocks, etc. at the still-lighted, second-story clothing store windows when most of the city was blacked out in order to make it a more difficult target in case the Japanese decided to drop bombs on the mainland. As I recall, it was a little bit scary driving without headlights. The view of a blacked-out city from the upper porch of my home at 4523 5th Ave. N.E. was a scene of beauty and wonder.

Within the week, Bob Kiebler (KIA 12/7/44) and I went downtown to the Exchange Building when the Navy held its tests for prospective aviation cadets. The mental exams were easy, and both Bob and I were instructed to report the following day for our physical exams. Bob flunked out almost at once due to an irregular heartbeat. Two days later, having just successfully completed the tough physical exam that my friend couldn't pass, I was told that I had failed the final exam. Kidneys again. Moreover, the Navy, in their infinite wisdom, would have nothing further to do with me, even though, as one medical officer pointed out, my specialty as a journeyman aircraft assembler was desperately needed. In retrospect, I'm happy for the Navy's arrogance, for if they had accepted me, I most assuredly would have spent the rest of the war repairing Navy airplanes in some god-forsaken hole in the South Pacific, or below decks on some aircraft carrier.

I went back to Boeing, while soon thereafter, the 41st Infantry Division headed overseas taking with it Stan and Bill and thousands of others for their rendezvous with destiny.

In September, I received my draft notice but thought little about it. I had already flunked out of the Army, and the Navy rejected me, so I didn't bother to advise my supervisors at Boeing. If I had, they would have insisted on a deferment as the production shops were critically short of skilled personnel at the time. I reported to the Draft Board but did not mention any physical problems. Consequently, I was listed as 1-A and ordered to appear for a physical. A Greyhound bus took a load of us to Tacoma and what passed for a physical was completed in about an hour. The standard joke in those days was that "one doctor looked down your throat while, at the same time, another doctor looked up your ass. If they couldn't see each other, you were in."

Amid the confusion of so many guys all taking a physical at the same time, I managed to switch my urine specimen with only God knows who, and so I passed. During the time needed to process the paperwork and the swearing-in ceremony, I went to a movie at some local theater: "At Last." It seemed appropriate at that time, as it still does in my memory, for *at last* I was going to be in the service.

Attack on Pearl Harbor
December 7, 1941

3

I boarded a bus loaded with other inductees for transportation to Fort Lewis where presumably all of us would soon be indoctrinated into the mysteries of Army life.

I returned to the Army Center at the designated hour, and together with fifty or sixty other guys, was sworn into the Army of the United States. The designation "United States Army" was reserved for regular Army personnel.

I was absolutely elated. I was in the Army! I didn't care what fate had in store for me. All I was certain of was that I wasn't going to spend the war working at Boeing. I was now a part of my own great rendezvous with destiny, whatever that might be.

One of the first things I did was to buy a candid camera, an Argus C-3 that cost the princely sum of twelve dollars, about ten percent of my monthly wages. That camera went with me halfway around the world, including combat after Normandy,

(I did not take it with me into Normandy), until it was lost in a blinding snowstorm somewhere in the Ardennes during the Battle of the Bulge. While many of the pictures I took in Holland survived, most were destroyed by enemy artillery fire. Of course, none of the pictures I took in the Ardennes survived.

Although I was inducted into the Army on October 20th, 1941, I did not actually report for active duty until November 1st, taking advantage of the Army's policy of granting time to clear up business and/or personal affairs. On that date, I boarded a bus loaded with other inductees for transportation to Fort Lewis where presumably all of us would soon be indoctrinated into the mysteries of Army life. And indeed, over the next few days, we managed to get a uniform, pull KP, and learn to fall in and out twenty times a day.

On the second day, we were marched to a huge hall to hear about such things as military courtesy, venereal disease, and other matters of interest that the Army deemed important. Somewhere along the way an officer said something to the effect that the Army was looking for volunteers for a new, tough, and dangerous special unit: the Paratroops. Participants had to weigh less than one-hundred-eighty pounds, be in excellent physical condition, young, tough, etc. Not a single person, out of the several hundred present, volunteered. The officer then commented: "No one? Well, we're batting 100% on *that* so far this week," and the entire audience roared with laughter. He then proceeded to talk about a few other matters, and finally we were dismissed.

I have no real recollection at what point I decided to go forward, but as the guys began filing out, I walked to the front of the auditorium and told the officer I would volunteer. Without comment, he turned to the table behind him, picked up a piece of paper, and handed it down to me. The paper simply said, "I will jump from an airplane in flight." I signed the paper and gave it back to him. He then asked me to hand up my Form 6. Immediately thereafter, my Form 6 was stamped with large red letters: PARATROOPS. At that precise moment, I became a marked man.

4

I didn't have a clue what I was getting in to, but I didn't care. Whatever fate had in store for me in the months ahead, I was confident I could handle.

To this day, I am not certain why I volunteered. Pride, I guess. I was still so chagrinned at having flunked both Army and Navy physicals that there was something of an "I'll show the bastards" attitude in signing that paper. But it was absurd: probably a classic example of pride getting in the way of judgement. I was for all intents and purposes unfit for military service; in the service under false pretenses, and volunteering for a branch of the service that required maximum physical condition and courage. Furthermore, I was terrified of heights, and at one hundred fifty pounds and six feet tall, was hardly a prototype paratrooper.

I had no sooner returned to the barracks when a sergeant called me out and told me to report to the dispensary for a special physical required of all would-be paratroopers. I was stunned! In the Army only two days and I had inadvertently put myself in position to again be put out of the service. Although it was probably the most thorough physical I had taken to date, a urinalysis apparently wasn't required. One of the doctors thought I had flat feet but didn't pursue that matter, and so I passed. The following day, I boarded a train that was to take me to Camp Blanding, Florida, near Jacksonville, to join the ranks of the fledgling 508 Parachute Infantry Regiment. I didn't have a clue what I was getting in to, but I didn't care. Whatever fate had in store for me in the months ahead, I was confident I could handle. And, strangely enough, I did with ease.

The long train trip across the country in the dead of winter was quite pleasant. I learned the fine art of three-handed pinochle, playing all day long with a couple of guys headed for the Army Air Corps in Miami. Occasionally, the train would stop, and all us new GI's would march around a block or two of some small town along the way. It was the route of the Great Northern Railroad, and I had actually traveled this same route in 1939 on my way to the New York World's Fair.

I have no recollection of the trip from Chicago south to Florida, but one beautiful, warm morning during the first week of November, I arrived at the small railroad station at Stark, Florida to view my first paratroopers, the cadre who were to make paratroopers of us all. But of the forty-five hundred who were processed, only twenty-three hundred of us survived basic training to reach jump school.

I can still remember the ride into camp in a truck atop our barracks bags to the catcalls of others along the way that had preceded us into basic training. All were "straight-legs" with little knowledge that a parachute regiment was being formed in their midst.

The 508 Parachute Infantry Regiment was constituted on October 20, 1942 and was to be the first of its kind formed from scratch to complete airborne basic training, move on to jump school, then to advanced training, and finally, overseas and combat in the European Theater of Operations.

In some ways, the program was designed to see how far they could push recruits. It was a grueling experience and it started with a visit to team doctors/psychiatrists who asked such questions as "Why do you want to be a paratrooper?" and/or, "Don't you know you'll be dead in six months?" To which I replied, "If it doesn't bother you, why should it bother me?" I was told to get the hell back to my company.

But while the basic training was physically and mentally demanding, there was seldom any of the nonsense depicted in most war movies where DI's are screaming at, and/or demeaning recruits. In our outfit you either measured up to airborne standards, or you were gone. We were almost always treated like men. The screening of recruits, the extreme discipline required, and the paratroop training program was apparently a huge success as nobody questions the fact that as a fighting unit, we were among the finest in the world. And from the very first day our officers and NCO's ran as we ran, marched as we marched, and in the field, ate as we ate, and generally lived as we lived.

5

As the weeks turned into months, then into years, long, tedious marches, often under absolutely terrible conditions, became routine and my beloved M-1 rifle but a toy in my hands.

Originally, I was assigned to Headquarters Company, 2nd Battalion that was then in the process of building up to full strength with new recruits arriving daily, most right out of the reception centers from across the country. Few had seen any previous military service.

As recruits, we were provided all the things we would need that had not been previously issued upon induction into the Army. The new items included the M-1 rifle, a bayonet, a canteen, a helmet, mess gear, etc.

When I first received the M-1 and the helmet, I thought they both weighed a ton and couldn't imagine ever getting used to either. Now, properly decked out, we were about to embark on a ten-mile march, M-1, helmet, and all. But I didn't think any of us were quite prepared for such an introduction to the infantry. Some dropped out after only a few miles, but most hobbled along on blistered feet, determined to stick it out. While I had no problems with my feet (notwithstanding that doctor at the reception center) I was near exhaustion toward the end, and with each grueling mile, my M-1 and steel helmet became unbearably heavy. As the weeks turned into months, then into years, long, tedious marches, often under absolutely terrible conditions, became routine, and my beloved M-1 rifle but a toy in my hands. The steel helmet somehow lost all its weight, becoming no more than a felt hat.

With basic training underway, we were subjected to daily five-mile "jogs" and an hour of calisthenics and/or judo. Almost every day, the group marched somewhere into and then out of the boondocks. We trained on small-unit tactics that, at our level, consisted mostly of running, crawling, digging, and/or fighting with one another, which included knocking the man around you down, and then dealing with the melee that ensued. Of course, we soon learned to play the game – especially if the guy you were supposed to knock down was Brightsman who I'll introduce you to in the next chapter. Strangely enough, some that was actually fun.

The only saving grace to all that was happening was that we didn't spend a lot of time on parade; the ground junk so dear to the hearts of chair-borne brass. Hell, we didn't even know what a "Retreat Formation" was (the lowering of the flag each evening) until nearly the end of the war. We almost never paraded, only enough to get by without looking like an unruly mob. I have a couple of great stories to tell on how we used to screw up a formation, and our post-Normandy review by Ike. But I won't get into that now.

Sometime around the fifth week, we began finding out how to fire our rifles. The stuff we went through prior to going out to the rifle range is so laughable, it's not worth mentioning. Mostly it was WWI type of training. The actual time at the range itself was a crashing bore. Mostly we spent time doing nothing until our turn came up to fire a few rounds at a target some few hundred yards away. Worse still, was our turn in the pits marking targets. A couple of days later, I was told I had qualified as an "expert." I'll never know how that came about, as I will always believe they got me confused with some other guy. While I could usually hit the target, I seriously doubt if I ever came near to the "bullseye." And the answer is simple: an M-1 is designed for neutral or right-eye firing. My left eye is the governing eye; hence, aiming with my right eye always resulted in considerable distortion. And you can't shoot an M-1 rifle from your left shoulder unless you want spent shell casings in your face as they eject.

But, for whatever reason, the dye was cast, and as an "expert rifleman," I found myself transferred to a rifle company. I didn't know it at the time, but the survival rate of those in a Headquarters Company was infinitely better than those of us in a rifle (line) company.

6

He could charm the gold out of a banker's teeth while
willingly giving him the shirt off his back. And he was
my constant companion for the next twenty-two months
until his death...

Soon after arriving in F Company, I was put on KP and there met a handsome young man named Gerald Brightsman. He had also qualified as an expert rifleman and had been transferred into F Company at the same time as me. In those early days, we had a First Sergeant who could not keep an accurate duty roster. As a consequence, when he lost track of duty assignments, he would simply start all over at the beginning of the alphabet. As there were only three in the company whose name began with the letter "A," and two of those were "acting" corporals, Broderick and Brightsman frequently found themselves pulling extra duty. One of the more obnoxious duties was KP, and the dirtiest job on KP was the pots and pans. And so he and I, in laughing defiance of another stupid day in the kitchen, always volunteered for the job. We became wonderful, warm and close friends, scrubbing large, greasy, messy pots and associated pans, on opposite sides of the huge metal tubs that had been designed for that purpose.

Gerald Brightsman was from The Dalles, Oregon, grew up in utter poverty, apparently without a father, but he had an uncle, "Scratch," whom he was very fond of. He worked in the wheat fields with the grown men, helping to support his mother and younger brother. He had graduated from The Dalles High School in 1939, and at the age of eighteen, had left home for Los Angeles to seek a better life. After arriving there, he had no trouble landing a job in a machine shop as he had a natural flair for the mechanical and could fix almost anything, skills learned during the depth of the Depression when all the farm equipment had to be kept running. In those days, there was seldom any money for new equipment or replacement parts. His teenaged years in the wheat fields made him incredibly strong, and on those rare occasions when his anger was aroused, very damn tough. But mostly, he was a warm, outgoing guy and made friends with everybody. Above all, he loved the ladies and would screw a woodpile if he thought a snake was in it.

It was great fun to watch him operate. He could charm the gold out of a banker's teeth while willingly giving him the shirt off his back. And he was my constant companion for the next twenty-two months until his death during an attack on the outskirts of the small Dutch town of Beek.

He and I had spent long hours talking and dreaming aloud of the great times we would have when the war was over. Neither of us had a very clear idea of what we were doing in the paratroops, but the potential for great danger was never of concern.

Even after all of these years, it is with immense sadness that I remember that time. A few days after the battle for Beek, Holland, I had the priveledge of being "burial sergeant." I led several of my men back to the area where my dear friend, along with Pat Rickard, Wade Smith, Chuck Logan, and a couple of others had fallen. As we looked down at what had been Gerald Brightsman, now just a discolored, stinking, maggot-infested corpse, many of the guys wept, and something went out of me that day.

Gerald Brightsman
(and friend)
Camp Mackall, N.C.
1943

7

At the crack of dawn, we fell out for roll call, and our first day at the parachute school began with all the excitement and, perhaps apprehension, that came with just being there.

Early in February, those of us that had survived the thirteen weeks of basic training boarded a train headed for Georgia that would take us to Fort Benning for jump school and whatever was to follow. I can tell you, we were a cocky, happy, confident bunch as we left Blanding. The physical hardening, jogging, and marching all day and night were accepted as part of the program, but the lousy food and no weekend liberties was the pits. If it hadn't been for the cookies, Fig Newtons, ice cream, and beer at the nearby PX, we'd all have starved to death.

We arrived at Fort Benning in the middle of a cold, very black night, and as we lined up ready to move out, the only thing clearly visible were the lights atop the two hundred fifty-foot training towers that we would be formally introduced to in a couple of weeks. No transportation had been provided for us, so we started on what turned out to be a very long march as we were carrying our packs, rifles, and other equipment. Our destination was known as the Frying Pan area of the Fort, but this was February. The oppressive heat of summer that had earned the Frying Pan its name and fearsome reputation, fortunately, was not a factor for us to deal with.

At the crack of dawn, we fell out for roll call, and our first day at the parachute school began with all the excitement and, perhaps apprehension, that came with just being there. Shortly after breakfast, the entire battalion marched down to Lawson Field and assembled on a small hillside to observe what we were told was to be some demonstration jumps that would be put on for us. During those early days, paratroopers jumped onto the Air Force's Lawson Field, but as the volume of activity increased, sometime later, the airfield ceased being the Drop Zone for trainees, as new and larger areas were created across the Chattahoochee River in Alabama. As we sat waiting, a single C-47 approached, and as it came over the Drop Zone, a lone "paratrooper" jumped. And, of course, the parachute failed to open and the victim plummeted to earth trailing what was known as a "streamer." Everybody laughed and cheered, much to the consternation of the school instructors that had now replaced our cadre sergeants. Nobody had been even slightly fooled. It was obvious that a dummy had been rigged for our benefit.

Alas, we were soon to pay for our arrogance, laughing at the school's little show. First, we had to run through the obstacle course twice and then double-time around the outskirts of the airfield for an hour or so. By lunch, the instructors began wishing they had never seen us, as almost to a man, we were in a lot better shape than they were. Blanding may have taken an awful toll, but those of us that had survived were in very good physical shape, so much so that the normal "A" Stage, consisting of a week of brutal physical conditioning, was waived for the entire regiment.

So, we began with what was known as "B" Stage – parachute packing and various static training devices that had been developed over time by the school's personnel. In those early days (February 1943 was still fairly early in the life of the parachute school) much of the training equipment was rather primitive by modern standards. Located immediately behind the packing sheds down on Lawson Field, the equipment consisted of a landing trainer; the sole purpose of which seemed to be an exercise in tumbling while hanging onto our risers when we hit the ground. I forgot once, and spent the rest of one morning jogging around the area hollering, "I will not drop my risers!" I later found out it was a very good idea to hang onto the risers until the parachute collapsed.

The other piece of equipment was what appeared to be a makeshift thirty-foot tower that, unlike the landing trainer, was a bit of a challenge for those of us who became nervous when more than five inches off the ground. We snapped on a standard parachute harness and jumped from a small door at the top of the tower while hooked to an overhead cable. The only problem was that the cable was rather slack and as you rode pell-mell down its incline, you had to remember to get your feet up before hitting the ground or risk a broken ankle or leg. I performed without any problems.

"B" Stage afternoons were devoted to learning how to pack the parachutes, that we would subsequently jump with, as a sort of confidence builder. We worked in pairs, and Brightsman would not permit anyone but me to be his packing partner, even though, after our first jump, we didn't always jump together. Generally, "B" Stage was not too bad of an experience.

On the following Monday, we marched down to the "C" Stage area and the three two hundred fifty-foot towers whose lights had greeted us upon our arrival. These were the same parachute towers that had been a major attraction at the 1939 New York City World's Fair, and I remember seeing them during my visit there that summer. My New York friend and I had no desire to take the chair ride up and down at the time. Too expensive and too scary. Those same towers continued to function for the Airborne for over fifty years, ever since they were purchased by the Army in 1941, without the chairs, to become part of the paratroop training program. Eventually determined to be obsolete, they were finally dismantled, I believe in the late eighties.

While the towers dominated the scene, there was one minor

side attraction that all of us got a chance to become familiar with. I can't remember if it had a name, but whatever it was called, some time later it was discarded as being too dangerous. Anyhow, the trainee donned a modified parachute harness and, while in a prone position, was lifted to a height of about twenty feet and, on command, pulled a ripcord. Then, while falling, changed the ripcord from right hand to left hand shouting, "One thousand, two thousand, three thousand". When it worked as it was intended, the trainee, still in a prone position, came to a sudden halt a couple of feet from the ground. I guess it didn't always work as intended...

We were separated into small groups below the towers, and ten to fifteen of us at a time would form around a steel circle that contained a complete parachute. A cable, lowered from an arm of the tower was then attached to the apex of the parachute. I don't remember how the thing worked, but work it did – beautifully. All I can remember is that as I was being pulled up to the release point, I could see all over Fort Benning. Once I was released from the mechanism, the descent was exactly the same as if I had jumped from an airplane, sans any opening shock. On the second "jump" I sprained my ankle pretty badly, same thing I had done while skiing years before, but I just had the medics tape it up. I hobbled around for a couple of days and got out of the daily hour of double timing. The landing procedure taught at the school during those early months resulted in a lot of sprains and/or broken bones before most of us learned how to land properly – no thanks to the Army. And, all through early training, we were forever practicing the proper way to tumble upon hitting the ground. Once into advanced training we NEVER again did any tumbling.

Actually, "C" stage was almost fun. The only problem was spending so much time doing nothing. Running a whole battalion through jump school each week strained the facilities to the limit. The entire 508 completed the course in three consecutive weeks: 1st Battalion, then 2nd Battalion (us,) followed by 3rd Battalion during the final week.

So, "C" Stage ended and the excitement began to mount as "D" Stage was on our schedule for the following week. To actually jump from an airplane in flight was suddenly becoming a reality. I don't remember exactly how I felt. I was proobably apprehensive, of course, but certainly not afraid. I don't think I was ever really afraid. But the truth is, I never in my wildest dreams thought I'd survive the physical and mental toughness that was required of special outfits like the paratroops and the rangers. Somehow I kept thinking that the Army would catch up with me and toss me out again. But here I was at Fort Benning at the parachute school, about to do the unthinkable.

8

---

*I simply cannot describe the thrill of that first jump.
I had apparently done everything right, for my parachute
snapped open with little more than a minor jolt, and as I
looked down, the earth came up to meet me.*

Monday arrived, and so did the weather. It had turned bitter cold, accompanied by strong winds and heavy rain. We did our usual hour of calisthenics and then set out for a tour of the base, often at the double, just to pass the time. The rest of the day, we just laid around.

Tuesday morning was a duplicate of Monday, but the afternoon was infinitely worse than Monday's was, as the Brass decided listening to military lectures and/or seeing military training films would keep our minds active. I always fell asleep during those, so I can't remember what they were about. But we were all bored to death and just wanted to get on with the damn program.

The weather cleared and the winds died down on Wednesday, so the company formed up and we double-timed down to Lawson Field. Brightsman and I grabbed the parachutes we had previously packed, helped each other put them on and then waddled out to the flight line and boarded the first aircraft we could find that had room for us. In those days, it was first come, first served. As we entered the cabin, we were directed to the bucket seats along the right-hand side of the aircraft. As we sat down, we looked across the aisle to the ten that had preceded us, and who we knew would jump before our side did.

And so we took off, everybody aboard with their own thoughts, most of us far more excited than nervous. As we circled Lawson Field, the jumpmaster ordered the "stick" sitting opposite us to "stand up and hook up." As we watched, I think spellbound, they went through the well-rehearsed procedure without a hitch. Then the green light flashed on and ten guys disappeared out of the door, one on top of another. None of that leg-tapping, go-go-go nonsense often seen in movies and/or TV.

And now it was our turn. The order "stand up and hook up" brought us to our feet. Brightsman was immediately in front of me, both of us in the middle of the "stick." We likewise sailed through the pre-jump procedure, and with the jumpmaster's, "Is everybody happy?" and our response, a rousing "Yes," the green light flashed on, and I followed Brightsman out the door. It was absolutely spectacular...

I simply cannot describe the thrill of that first jump. I had apparently done everything right, for my parachute snapped open with little more than a minor jolt, and as I looked down, the earth came up to meet me. I even landed without the expected body-jarring.

I had done it! I had jumped from an airplane in flight, and as luck would have it, everything had gone according to the book. As I gathered up my parachute and headed for the edge of the field where trucks awaited us, I think I walked about a foot off the ground.

On Thursday morning I made my second jump. The opening shock almost took my head off. Thursday afternoon, I made my third jump and took another pounding. Just to make sure I was under no misconception about military parachuting, I came in like a freight train on a backward oscillation and slammed through ice-covered casual water left over from the earlier rainstorms. But what the hell, Brightsman and I were up and at 'em on Friday to make our fourth jump into a minor rainsquall. Believe it or not, Brightsman and I packed our semi-wet parachutes and jumped again Friday afternoon without any ill effects. We just wanted to get it over with, damp chutes or not, as the weather seemed to be deteriorating and we wanted that fifth and qualifying jump without any further delays. Ironically, Saturday's weather turned out to be just fine, but what the hell, our qualifying jumps were on record as of Friday.

Saturday afternoon Brigadier General Howell presented us

our wings and gave us a brief speech to the effect that we were about to embark on a journey that would take us to some foreign shore to do battle with our country's enemies, and that as paratroopers, much would be expected of us. To prepare us for that task, we would now enter into advanced training for those battles that were sure to come, or some such sort of pep talk.

Well, I was a paratrooper! A 4-F in a 1-A outfit. What a laugh, but, man, I felt great! I had actually done the unthinkable. I had survived the rigors of Blanding, made five parachute jumps, and was now a member of a very special, dangerous, and elite group that in effect said to the world that I was willing to risk my life while soldiering with the Army's finest. As time went on, however, I came to realize it was all just so much BS, particularly after Normandy.

9

While I am sure my mother was quite proud of me, she continued to plead with me to get into something less dangerous. My father never said a word, one way or another.

It was now time for a well-earned furlough, but some of us from the West Coast were concerned that the ten days allotted would not give us sufficient time to get home and back. One of the men asking for travel time turned out to be from Seattle. And so I met Jim Jackman, who for a variety of reasons, missed most of our time at Blanding. In what turned out to be an "it's a small world" coincidence, we discovered that he and I had attended Lincoln High School together for three years and graduated in the same class of '39, yet until that afternoon at Fort Benning, had never before met. Not surprisingly, as there were six hundred two members in that graduating class. After jump school, Jimmy and I almost always jumped together, up to and including Normandy, and I still have fond memories of the times we had.

My brief visit home was pleasant, but boring. All my friends were gone, and with gas rationing, it was difficult to get around. I did manage to attend a dance at the Trianon Ballroom (*the* dance hall in Seattle.) I can't remember what orchestra was playing that night but it was one of the "Big Bands" of that time. The place was absolutely jammed, the dance floor so packed that the couples seldom even attempted to dance. They just stood around listening to the music. As I recall, there were at least a million sailors, (Seattle was known as a Navy town) a handful of soldiers and few pretty girls.

Those few days I was home, I noticed that everywhere I went people stared at me. I often just wore a field jacket that displayed a large patch, a white parachute on a blue background, that had UNITED STATES PARATROOPS in large white letters encircling it. That jacket, together with my cap containing the same patch, and my jump boots, presented a very different kind of soldier, rarely seen west of the Mississippi.

At one point, my mother and I were doing some shopping in the University District when some kids spotted me and started yelling, "There's a guy from the parachute battalion." While I am sure my mother was quite proud of me, she continued to plead with me to get into something less dangerous. My father never said a word, one way or another.

A day or two later, I again boarded a train for the long trip back across the country to Fort Benning where we would begin the next phase of our instruction, laughingly called "advanced" training.

Immediately after all of the 2nd Battalion had returned from furlough, we headed north to an all-new airborne training center, Camp Mackall, located about thirty miles from Fort Bragg, North Carolina. At the time of our arrival, the contractors had just completed the building that we were to occupy, so for the next few weeks we did nothing but pick up the mess the construction workers had left behind. While all of the roads (unpaved in company area)s were in, it became our task to construct sidewalks, small border fences, and other stuff to make the place a bit more liveable. Again, we were housed in relatively small "hutments" of about thirty men each. Bunk beds lined each side of the quarters. There was no special lodging for senior NCO's, but each guy had shelf space, a clothes rack, and a wooden foot locker. We had now assumed a measure of civilized existence. When we weren't beautifying the place, we went out on fire patrol specifically to address the ones burning in several areas of the pine forests that surrounded the entire camp.

Mackall was so new that when we arrived, reliable bus transportation had not yet been provided for. Consequently, most of the enlisted personnel were stuck in camp over the weekends. But even after the busses began operating they only went as far as Rockingham and Hamlet, both at that time small, stupid southern towns. But it didn't matter as most of the time we were in the boondocks ten to twelve hours a day and/or night, marching, crawling, running, digging, and sweating while carrying our weapons and the other equipment so dear to the hearts of the infantrymen. I hate to think how many times my thoughts returned to those Washington National Guard Infantrymen of long ago that I thought were nuts and concluded that I was the one that was nuts.

Soon after arriving at Camp Mackall, I made PFC, and along with about half of the company, received the Good Conduct Medal. It now seems laughable, but in the old military establishments, being awarded a GCM was considered a bit of an honor. Oh, well, it was my first medal.

Home on furlough, fresh out of jump school
March, 1943

Ann, our hero, and Dad
March, 1943

I was overwhelmed by all them stripes!
March, 1943

With Mom
March, 1943

508th Parachute Infantry Regiment
United States Army

This is to Certify That:

Robert James Broderick

has satisfactorily completed the prescribed course in Parachute Packing, Ground Training, and has made the required number of Parachute Jumps from a plane in flight. He is, therefore, rated from this date March 7, 1943 as a qualified Parachutist

Ray E. Lindquist

Colonel, 508th Parachute Infantry
Commanding

10

To this day, I have absolutely no recollection of how I came to be promoted, or who it was that informed me that I was a corporal.

Brightsman and I were put on "special assignment" as lifeguards at a small lake in the flight path of the aircraft bringing paratroops in for their drop on a field about a half-mile away. The guys jumping were from other outfits. We were just on temporary duty to make sure nobody drowned if they landed in the lake. For a couple of weeks, all we did was lay on our butts and watch the fly-over and parachute drops – rather exciting at first, but after a couple of days, we became totally disinterested as none of the paratroopers landed close to the lake. Apparently Brightsman and I did such a wonderful job as lifeguards that we were able to continue, but this time at a creek that was about thirty feet wide and up to four feet deep in the middle. To add realism to the "river" crossing, some officer supplied us with Cherry Bombs that we tossed around our guys wading through the creek, which of course, really pissed them off. It should be noted that the lake, the creek, and damn near all other visible sources of water, rapidly disappeared as the temperature skyrocketed, so our valuable services as life guards vanished right along with them.

A short time later, I landed in the base hospital as a brief influenza epidemic spread throughout the camp. I had a high temperature for a few days, but no other problems, including kidneys, so I assumed that whatever had bugged me in the past was now history, and I began thinking about the cadets again.

I believe it was some time during May that word came down from Airborne Command that volunteers would be accepted for immediate duty overseas. Considering my frame of mind and my growing hatred with everything the infantry represented, I figured anything was better than what we were currently doing. So I talked Brightsman into coming with me to see the company commander about volunteering. The 1st Sergeant acknowledged our request, but we were not allowed to see the captain. A short time later, Brightsman found himself among those slated for overseas shipment, but my name was not on the list. He was all packed and ready to go when the list was cut in half and he actually ended up staying. But those that did leave included our current platoon sergeant. So, George Menter moved up from squad leader sergeant to fill the vacant position.

Corporal Jim Lanham moved up to squad leader sergeant, and I became a corporal.

To this day, I have absolutely no recollection of how I came to be promoted, or who it was that informed me that I was now a corporal. I'm reasonably certain that my former National Guard duty may have been a factor, but I'm inclined to believe my having scored a relatively high number on the Army IQ examination was probably of considerable importance in the final decision. There were about thirty PFCs in the company at the time, presumably all eligible for promotion. Our senior officers, all West Pointers, insisted that the Army was run by NCOs, hence there apparently was some other criteria for those who might be excellent soldiers but lacked whatever the brass looked for in the selection process. One of the continuing complaints coming from generals of regular infantry outfits was that Rangers, Paratroops, and Special Forces were taking the lion's share of the bright guys. Actually, every branch of the Army became "selective", leaving what was left for the regular infantry.

The new corporal and Brightsman
What usually happppened to me after giving
him an order...

11

---

*We would horse race out the door, sometimes riding
the parachute of the man in front...at least once in my
memory, I hit the side of the aircraft, proof positive I'd
made a very poor exit.*

By mid-May, the weather began to change and started to get
very warm. As the weeks slipped by, bringing us into summer, the
heat and humidity intensified to make the life of an infantryman
even more miserable. Those of us from the West Coast really
suffered, as we had never experienced humidity before. Getting
our brains beat out in the scorching heat, burning sand, fleas,
mosquitoes, snakes, lousy food, and no place to go on weekends
was our usual fare. As far as I was concerned, it was bloody awful,
and I can't think of a single redeeming feature of those long
tedious months of advanced training that somehow managed
to drag by in utter boredom and monotony.

From time to time there were a few breaks in the routine. Some of us managed to learn the secret of boarding the "Silver Meteor" without a ticket and riding that hundred-mile-an-hour streamliner into Washington D.C. in just a few hours. The local trains took up to thirty hours to travel the same distance, making a weekend in D.C. impossible. I had some great times there. You know, sightseeing, attending prayer meetings, and washing dishes at the local Salvation Army headquarters. Unfortunately, trips to D.C. were rather infrequent on an enlisted man's pay.

Some of the things we engaged in while learning how to be effective and efficient killers beat the hell out of marching around in the boondocks. We spent more time firing various light weapons, other than the M-1 rifle, but surprisingly far less than expected. As a corporal, I was armed with a Thompson submachine gun and became very proficient with it. It was an excellent assault weapon, but useless at much more than twenty yards. I spent a few days at demolition school where I learned all I needed to know about high explosives like C-2, TNT, and plastics; accessories such as caps, primer cord, shaped charges, etc. Some of the lessons learned were put to good use later during the many lulls in the fighting when it was worth your life to have a fire; a marble-sized hunk of C-2 (or shaved TNT) could be used to heat a cup of coffee without any noticeable flame showing.

During the months at Mackall, we managed to get in a mere five daytime and two nighttime jumps, albeit one of the night jumps was in Tennessee during maneuver. We spent a couple of weeks in South Carolina freezing our asses off, as it never seemed to stop raining and we had no rain gear. Besides, the entire time was spent as regular infantry, there to defend against an airborne attack by another parachute outfit. I wasn't very happy with any of it.

We made a couple of daytime jumps that were generally small affairs, battalion-size at best. As time went on, we participated in jumps involving the entire regiment. When we jumped at night over England, the entire division was involved. Thus, in a little more than a year, we went from what amounted to a few aircraft in the air during daylight hours, dropping a few hundred of us, to hundreds of aircraft at night dropping thousands of us. Some of our jumps during the early spring months were almost fun compared to those later on when we were burdened with the tools for survival. Other than our weapons, we had virtually no other equipment to contend with. We would horse race out the door, sometimes riding the parachute of the man in front. I found out that walking across another's canopy was like walking across a feather mattress; and, for an instant or so, see the tail of the aircraft fly over my head as I fell. At least once in my memory, I hit the side of the aircraft, proof positive I'd made a very poor exit.

And of course, there was the weather. Some of those jumps during the hot humid spring and summer were both amusing and dangerous. When temperatures reached into the nineties, with a humidity to match, a parachute could become very unpredictable in its descent. Once I floated down so gently that I was trying to feel for the ground as my parachute fluttered overhead, while similar thermal up drafts were keeping some other guys still high up in the air, climbing their risers trying to get down.

At another time, we flew through a rainsquall as we were jumping. It was like being thrown into a shower. On my first night jump, I was the last man in the stick, and as the entire stick could exit the aircraft in seconds the last man was virtually running out the door. I guess I was running as I dove out. Anyhow, I must have been upside down when my parachute opened as the connector-links crunched my helmet and knocked me out cold. The medics put a tag on me and I got a free ride back to camp. In Tennessee, I came in backwards and plowed through a whole field of dried cornstalks before I could get my parachute collapsed. I had landed reasonably close to the DZ while many others were dropped all over the mountains of Tennessee, resulting in a lot of serious injuries.

Mostly, though, we came down fast and hard. There were always accidents and injuries of one kind or another, especially during night jumps. But day or night there were always problems of running into one another, often collapsing one of the parachutes, or tangling with another's suspension lines, often ultimately resulting in injury to one or both jumpers. Other dangers came from stealing another's air, brassieres, blown panels, and slamming into walls, fences, barns, houses, rocks, or hanging up in trees. Those big twenty-eight foot canopies were uncontrollable, even if you could see where you were about to land, attempting to avoid some hazard below.

But it wasn't all bad, at least early on it wasn't. Most of the daytime jumps into reasonably good DZs were pretty much injury free. Broken legs or ankles were about all that might happen but even those relatively minor injuries were uncommon when we were dropped where we were supposed to be dropped.

Once the regiment unwittingly put on a show of sorts. A routine daylight jump was scheduled and my platoon's objective was to capture the small railway station at Hoffman, N.C. It was a beautiful spring day. We jumped, assembled, and moved from the DZ toward the station that was only about a mile or so away. As we arrived, surrounded, and took up positions at the objective, we were amused to notice that every window in the local passenger train was crammed with passengers watching as flight after flight of aircraft thundered directly overhead at seven hundred feet to drop paratroopers on the DZ we had just come from. Actually, it was a thrilling sight and those passengers who were in the windows to watch probably will remember it all their lives.

Broderick, Brightsman, and Chestnut
"Advanced Training"
1943

Brightsman and friend
More advanced training
Candor, N.C., 1943

12

---

*While each and every jump was unique, the jump itself
was simply a means to an end; to get us on the ground
ready to fight.*

Some things stick I in my memory. The evening of our night jump in Tennessee, we had to march from our bivouac area to the airfield, and in so doing, we passed a German prisoner of war compound. The Germans were standing in small groups behind the barbed wire fence silently watching as we passed. There was not a sound other than that of our marching boots. But they knew who we were, as only paratroopers wore the distinctive tan jump suits. I couldn't help but wonder what they must have been thinking so far from home, behind barbed wire, knowing with certainty that we were destined to kill many of their countrymen.

While each and every jump was unique, the jump itself was

simply a means to an end; to get us on the ground ready to fight. And once there, we were just lightly armed infantry assigned objectives that presumably would help the regular infantry accomplish much larger ones. But we seldom made actual parachute drops, so our time was spent ground-pounding like any other infantry outfit. And ground-pound we did, day after day, ad nauseum.

It was during one of these days in July, the temperature in the nineties and the humidity to match, that a small L-type "spotter" aircraft flew by our column at near ground level. The pilot appeared to be wearing a bathing suit and his baseball-type hat clearly showed the silver bar of a 1st Lieutenant. The bastard was smiling at us as he sped by, and he looked cool and comfortable as if he enjoyed what he was doing. I was so pissed I would have shot him if I'd had any ammunition in my Thompson. (Just kidding...I wouldn't have done that.) But whoever that lieutenant was, he did trigger in me a decision to get the hell out of the infantry and into the Air Force. Nobody could take the physical punishment we took every damned day and not be in excellent shape. So when we returned to camp, I wrote a brief letter to the Army Air Force in Washington D.C. I didn't tell anyone what I was up to. I knew enough about how the game was played to be certain my request wouldn't get by the 1st Sergeant had I attempted to go through proper channels.

With the letter posted, I went on furlough. I didn't want another long slow train ride to Seattle, so I went over to the packing sheds and checked out a T-7 parachute and hitched a ride in a C-47 to Fort Benning. From Benning, I had a wild ride in an A-20 to Atlanta. I don't think we ever got much above the trees all the way down. At the airport in Atlanta, I waited around all morning, together with a Navy Ensign and a Marine 2nd Lieutenant, both just out of flight school at Pensacola and trying to hitch a ride west, same as I. Finally, in the late afternoon, a B-24 came in and the captain agreed to take the two officers, but saying he was overloaded, would not take me. My two friends then interceded on my behalf and the captain reluctantly agreed.

For the take-off, the three of us stood on the main support beam in the bomb bay as all others aboard were jammed up front in order to get as much weight forward as possible.

A short time after we were airborne, the crew chief laughingly told us that because the aircraft engines were burning eighty-seven octane gas instead of one hundred, the engines lacked sufficient power to lift the heavily overloaded aircraft with the ease that the higher gas would have provided. He said we had just barely cleared some trees as the pilots tried to gain altitude, and he added, it was the closest encounter with disaster he had ever experienced after years of flying before adding, "The skipper may be a bit crazy, but he's a damn good pilot." Standing in the bomb bay, we had had no inkling of any problem, other than no place to sit during take-off.

Somewhere between Atlanta and Fort Worth, some of those

on the flight engaged in a bit of horizontal refreshment with a big, fat, ugly WAC who was also aboard. The Marine and I were sleeping in the rear of the aircraft when the Ensign woke us up and asked if we wanted a turn at the fun and games, as the WAC was apparently generous to a fault in dispensing her favors. The cabin lights were on, and the sweet thing was sitting there stark naked, but I'd have to be a Hemingway to really describe the scene. We thanked the Ensign for his attention, but we both declined the honor...

13

Dad told me that a telegram from the Air Force had been relayed from the regiment to the house ordering me to report to Pope Field... I had actually beat the system.

From Fort Worth, I flew out to Phoenix for one of the most tortuous landings I've every experienced. No longer in the B-24, and sans most of those who had been in the flight from Atlanta, I was now in a familiar C-47. As we approached Phoenix and began our decent, it started to become very warm inside the airplane and thermal updrafts began buffeting it to such an extent that it became prudent to hang on to the bucket seats. After two separate attempts to get the airplane down, the pilot finally dove for the runway and succeeded. Everyone on board was soaking wet by the time we taxied up to the operations shack. Some smart ass kid driving a weapons carrier out to pick up the officer's luggage said to the pilot, "Congratulations, sir.

That was the best landing we've seen all day." The sweat-soaked pilot was not amused. At any rate, we continued westward and finally landed at a fighter base near Santa Ana, California. I thought hitching a ride north to Seattle would now be easy. But I was soon to learn that I was at a dead end as there seldom were any flights from the base anywhere north of Los Angeles.

I called home and told my folks that it looked like I was stuck in California and that I would try to get in touch with Tom. Dad told me that a telegram from the Air Force had been relayed from the regiment to the house ordering me to report to Pope Field, Fort Bragg, North Carolina by such-and-such a date. Dad then had a copy sent to me in care of the Western Union office on the base. I received the copy an hour or so later. I then returned to the operations shack where I showed the telegram to a pilot who said he'd fly me to another base near Santa Monica where he thought I might have a better chance for a ride north.

I still have a vivid memory of that trip. We went out to the flight line and boarded an AT-6 for the relatively short jaunt to Santa Monica. An AT-6 was used extensively by the military for all kinds of advanced training, (there are still hundreds of them around) but I didn't know that at the time. So we took off, and once we were over Los Angeles at about five thousand feet the pilot began putting that little airplane into every conceivable maneuver in the books. From time to time he would tell me to take the controls and follow his instructions. Mostly I remember him shouting at me over the intercom, with more than a few choice words thrown in for emphasis.

Then he would take the controls back and we'd be all over the sky again. I started to get airsick but managed to hang on until we landed. I thanked the pilot for trying to get me a bit closer to home but didn't think much of him as an instructor.

Santa Monica was, unforunately, just another dead end. So I got in touch with Tom, who was stationed somewhere in the vicinity, and we agreed to get together the following day.

That evening I ventured to the Hollywood district and wandered around with a million other service men, almost all Air Force cadets. I had a brief encounter with a couple of MP's who demanded to see my furlough papers before finally crapping out someplace.

I spent a couple of very pleasant days with Tom before boarding a train for the long trip back to camp. For whatever reason, my big brother was a pretty straight arrow, i.e. no booze or broads. I don't know what the hell he did for fun.

I no sooner arrived back in camp when the CQ told me to report to the battalion where, as it turned out, I got a real ass-chewing from the commander, but was issued, reluctantly I might add, a three day pass with orders to report to Pope Field for the Aviation Cadet examinations.

I had actually beat the system.

Tom, now a Warrant Officer

Robert J. Broderick, now with two stripes.
Long Beach, CA
1943

14

Those were momentous years and I wanted a part of the action. But I must confess... I sometimes wondered what I was doing there when I probably didn't have to be.

On the appointed day, I checked in at the Air Force facilities at Pope Field and was surprised to note that the accommodations were nothing like what the infantry provided. There were sheets and pillowcases on the beds and curtains on the windows. At breakfast the following morning, a young airman on KP asked me how I wanted my eggs, and for a fleeting moment thought he was being sarcastic. But when I said "over easy," I got eggs over easy. And there was milk and butter and salt and pepper and a tablecloth on the table and curtains on the mess-hall windows for crying out loud! I thought I was in a different world.

After breakfast, a couple dozen of us took some kind of examination to see how smart we were. It was easy and I finished early on. The next day, most of us reported to the dispensary for what I thought would be a routine physical. Of course I flunked out; kidneys again. A medical staff sergeant politely told me I could apply for a medical discharge and be out of the Army. In a rather arrogant manner, I told him that if the results of my physical got back to my regiment I'd come back and pay him a visit. He told me that he didn't give a damn if I stayed in the Army forever and to get the hell out of his dispensary. As things turned out, no report came back to the regiment as far as I knew.

So much for my longing to become a pilot. I was absolutely defeated. Here I was in the kind of outfit that demanded top physical condition and I couldn't pass a damned physical.

When I arrived back at camp, nobody said a word to me; not my company commander, nor Lieutenant Gillespe, nor George Menter. I was not asked where I'd been or what I'd been up to. While I was certain I would be busted down to a buck private as soon as I got back, nothing happened. All I got out of the whole damn affair was that for some reason my kidneys continued to mysteriously malfunction, and knowing that, it influenced my decision a couple months later to decline an opportunity to go to Officer Candidate school at Fort Benning, for I would certainly face another physical there and would not be able to talk my way out of a medical discharge again.

Fate certainly plays strange tricks. Here it is, fifty-some odd years later, and I'm probably in better shape than most men my age, but at that time, presumably had such a life-threatening medical problem that I could thrive on great physical demands almost daily, but was not physically fit enough to sit on my big fat ass while "driving" an airplane. Even so, being a dogface infantryman was still better than spending the war years working at Boeing. At least, that's what I thought at the time. Those were momentous years and I wanted a part of the action. But I must confess that from time to time during those long, terrible months in combat, I sometimes wondered what I was doing there when I probably didn't have to be.

In December, we finally departed Camp Mackall for Camp Kilmer, New Jersey and for shipment overseas, arriving just before Christmas. We were stripped of all identification as paratroops. We even had to wear regular infantry canvas leggings, and continued to do so for a time, even after we landed in Ireland.

During the evening of December 28, 1943, the entire regiment was ferried down the Hudson River to a pier somewhere along Manhattan's west side and there boarded the USS James Parker, a banana boat that was to take us overseas to our immediate destination, as yet unknown to us. And for such a gala affair, we were honored by the presence of those wonderful ladies of the Red Cross who supplied us with coffee, donuts, and soft drinks...and a lot of beautiful, warm smiles.

Actually, the Parker was a very nice ship that, in peacetime, accommodated any number of tourists and other passengers between the United States and Latin America. Officers' quarters, while a bit crowded, were pretty nice compared to enlisted quarters, typically stuffed into the lower decks in tiers seven feet high. But nobody seemed to mind – we were finally on our way.

The USS James Parker eased out of New York harbor sometime during the night, slipping down the Hudson to join a convoy forming up off the coast. It was icy cold on deck, so most of us missed the move out-bound past the Statue of Liberty and out to sea. But I shall never forget, nor can I put into words, how I felt some long, weary months later as the USS Argentina silently moved *up* the Hudson River late at night *toward* a "brown-out" New York City. The decks were crowded with returning GI's, but not a sound was heard until we came upon the Statue of Liberty looming against the dark skyline. And a single voice from somewhere said, "There she is," and I thought, *I made it – I actually made it back!*

508th Parachute Infantry Regiment

A REGIMENT OF THE EIGHTY-SECOND AIRBORNE DIVISION

1st Lt. Fred E. Gillespie
Passing over Camp Mackall
1943

1st Lt. Fred E. Gillespie
Passing over Camp Mackall
1943

15

Captain Flanders was, for more reasons than I can count, the best damn company commander in the entire regiment. Unfortunately, he was killed on D-day.

Our trip across the ocean to Ireland took about ten days. Out in the middle of the North Atlantic, we were surprised when it became warm and pleasant up on deck. After the war, my brother John, who had spent a good deal of time on convoy duty aboard the battleship USS Alabama, told me ours was moving through some part of the Gulf Stream, hence the great weather in the dead of winter. Because it was so pleasant on deck, a lot of guys simply slept up there. And so, under beautiful star-filled skies and calm seas, Brightsman and I spent much of our time leaning over the rail and watching the beauty of the ship's wake, wondering aloud what the future had in store for us, never doubting that we would both return home safely.

Finally, we arrived at the huge harbor of Belfast, Ireland. After hours of delay, we disembarked unto that land of my father, albeit Protestant, North Ireland. Funny little trains were waiting to take us to the Port Rush area, and there, on the Lord of the Manor's estate, we settled into Quonset huts for our brief stay in that lovely land. It was there that we learned that we had been attached to the 82nd Airborne Division. At the time, it meant nothing to us.

A week or so after we arrived, I was walking through the area when I noticed what appeared to be a rather tall, slim, young lieutenant approaching. But even in the gloom of an Irish afternoon, the flash of silver on his cap did not seem just right. As I saluted this very handsome young man I noted, not the silver bar of a 1st Lieutenant, but the Silver Star of a General Officer. He returned my salute and we both continued on our solitary ways. It wasn't until a few hours later that I was informed that I had encountered, for the first time, Brigadier General James M. Gavin, Asstistant. Commander, 82nd Airborne Division. I was to see this remarkable man many times over the next fifteen months, both while in camp and during combat.

We had only been in Ireland a short time when, for reasons unknown, Jim Lanham suddenly snapped. He got very drunk, stole a jeep, was apprehended, arrested, and sent home. I then took his place as the squad leader sergeant of 12 men and Don Wright moved up as the assistant squad leader corporal.

North Ireland is very much like Seattle during those cold,

rainy and miserable months of January and February. Most of the Irish were warm and friendly, but occasionally we ran into anti-British sentiment – once by a farmer wielding a pitch-fork as we crossed one of his fields.

Jim Jackman and I spent a couple of days in Belfast, and Brightsman and I spent some weekends in Londonderry, although both cities were off-limits (too many opportunities to raise hell.) While there were the usual MP's in those cities, they were probably instructed to ignore us. Not so our own "chute patrol." MP's were not allowed in areas dominated by paratroops. Brightsman and I were arrested in Coleraine after it was put off limits. At the time we were passing through the place after visiting with a couple of nice young ladies at a little crossroad settlement farther up the coast. Of course we were hauled up before our company commander who gave us an ass-chewing, wanting to know what we'd been up to. As I started to explain, he broke into a big grin and said, "Okay, okay, you're dismissed." Captain Flanders was, for more reasons than I can count, the best damn company commander in the entire regiment. Unfortunately, he was killed on D-day. Needless to say, us Rover Boys avoided Coleraine on future ventures up the coast.

I can't remember having very much time to just relax long enough to enjoy our new surroundings. The regiment kept us busy almost all the time, and they worked the hell out of us, mostly at night. While we assumed we were carrying out our primary objective of securing some target and holding it until friendly forces arrived, for us it was just "digging in" from one place to another. In Ireland, in the dead of winter, it was just cold, wet and miserable.

Soon after I assumed my role as squad leader, the battalion commander "lifted" one of my men's rifles as he lay sleeping at the bottom of his foxhole. That was an extremely serious matter, and I could very well have been busted, but before it even got to my level, I had taken my squad on a long tortuous night problem. We arrived at all the "check points" and brought the entire squad back to camp at dawn. I was among the squad leaders to successfully do so. Apparently, the rifle incident blew over as I got my third stripe.

Our stay in Ireland didn't last long, for in early March we boarded those funny little trains again and returned to Belfast to embark for parts unknown. Actually, I can't remember sailing from Ireland to Scotland, but I do remember the stunning beauty of our travel up the Firth of Clyde to Glasgow. We unloaded at some small seaport town late in the evening and again boarded a train that took us through Glasgow and then south to our new home in the city of Nottingham, England, arriving sometime around midnight. Their double-deck busses and trucks waited to take us the few miles to Wollaton Park.

How can I possibly describe our stay in Nottingham and do it the justice it deserves? It was absolutely unbelievable and like nothing we had ever experienced before or since. The period from mid-March to June 3rd and from July 10th to September 14th was like a grand, prolonged vacation from the normal rigors of infantry life. To begin with, we were stationed in a park complete with beautiful grounds, a small lake and golf course, the King's deer and a castle looming over the entire area. We were housed in six-man tents, complete with cement slabs for the floors and a small potbellied stove that was primarily used for reheating food either scrounged from the mess hall or fish and chips from town. Downtown Nottingham was only minutes away via the buses that stopped outside the main gate. Beeston, a suburb of Nottingham, was only a few blocks from the park via the back wall, a very old eight-foot stone wall that surrounded the entire park where Brightman and I spent a good deal of our free time. There were no military training areas anywhere near and very few British troops within miles. The only Americans were some black service troops that never ventured into our area, or the city for that matter.

So, we found ourselves in a comparatively large English city where there were lots of pretty girls, plenty of booze, and absolutely wonderful people to make our stay more comfortable. Who said life ain't fair?

The "Castle"
Wollaton Park, Nottingham, England
1944

16

---

*About this time, we made our first night jump over England.
It turned out to be a complete fiasco... That night jump was,
in many respects, a forerunner of Normandy.*

Under the circumstances, it was tough trying to act like
soldiers. The first crisis developed almost at once. Some of
the clodheads in the regiment, mighty hunters probably from
New York city, began shooting the deer both for fun and extra
rations, I would guess. The English, however, took a very dim
view of such barbaric conduct and soon the remaining deer
were rounded up and transported to safety.

Within a couple of weeks, the colonel called the whole
regiment together and informed us that from now on we were
going to start acting like soldiers. He was tired of his men
stumbling back to camp at all hours of the night, so from then
on, there would be a midnight curfew instituted; guards would

be posted and the curfew strictly enforced. Everybody groaned. Then he told us a few hundred other things we were going to start doing and finally finished with, "One other thing, I want all of those women out of your tents. I don't give a damn if you guys screw yourselves to death. I can't afford to feed them."

A few more weeks passed and the colonel again called us all together. This time, the ass-chewing went something like this: "What the hell kind of outfit am I commanding? How are you going to fight the Germans when most of you can't even get back into camp after curfew without being caught by your own guards?" An absolute howl of glee went up, but he was dead serious and things started tightening up a bit. What really did the trick was the simple fact that the pubs ran out of their booze ration by ten o'clock and it didn't take two hours to kiss your girl goodnight and get back to camp on time. Besides, it was no big deal evading the guards if you really wanted to.

One other rather humorous, but deadly serious, problem was that for a long time we had a full combat load of ammunition and demolition under our cots. How we got through that period without blowing up the park, I'll never know. Even so, some nuts were always firing their weapons or trying to blow something up or down with C-2. And this in camp, of all places. But cooler heads eventually prevailed, especially when the regimental adjutant threatened a ten mile march with full packs "if another shot was fired." But he never carried out his threats, even though sporadic firing kept up for quite awhile.

By mid-April, we began a whole series of night problems. Loaded into trucks, but more often those double-decked buses, and taken somewhere out in the country, few of us had a clue what the hell was going on. At our level, I suppose it didn't matter. Mostly, whatever it was we were doing was for the benefit of senior officers. Actually, we came and went so many times that the people of Nottingham had no way of knowing that when we finally left for Normandy, it was for real.

About this time, we made our first night jump over England. It turned out to be a complete fiasco. All I remember about that night was the pilot telling Lieutenant Cook he wasn't exactly sure where the DZ was, but thought he could get us close and asked if we wanted to jump, or go back with him to the airfield. He apparently knew where that was! So, what the hell... We jumped.

When my chute opened, I remember seeing what appeared to be a farmhouse below, and as best I could, I slipped away from it and landed in a small open field along with three or four others in the stick. We were lucky. All of us had missed what turned out to be thick, thorny, ancient hedgerows that seemed to be everywhere in that area. I can guarantee that anyone slamming into those things would end up in the hospital. Lieutenant Cook finally rounded up all the guys and it was concluded that we were far from any recognized DZ. So, in typical Cook fashion, he said, "Screw it. Get some sleep".

At dawn, he sent scouts out in several directions, eventually finding out where we were, which was about ten miles from our intended DZ. Later that afternoon, we rejoined what had been a widely scattered company, and regiment, for that matter.

That night jump was, in many respects, a forerunner of Normandy. We lost Angel, Walton, Hamilton, Alexik, and a couple of replacements, mostly to broken legs. Like us, they had been dumped all over the countryside. Several planeloads were so far off course that the guys were dropped on a RAF bombing range that the British were bombing that night. A joke soon made its rounds that those that survived deserved combat pay. Nobody was killed.

17

Suddenly, a green light flashed on in the dome of an aircraft far ahead and, a split second later, our green light flashed on. I hollered, "Let's go!" and jumped out into the blackness.

The use and misuse of Airborne troops in the ETO are now well documented. Airborne operations were incredibly complex, especially at night, yet troop carrier pilots were often at the bottom rung of the ladder; inexperienced and poorly trained for the job they were supposed to do. Two serious, even disastrous, results followed. The first was the Air Force's inability to drop the majority of the troops when they were supposed to be dropped. Failing that, the ability for paratroops to assemble at night as a cohesive fighting unit was compromised. No matter how fast the stick could clear the aircraft, there was always uneven disbursement. Loaded down with guns, ammunition, demolition, mines, and all the other paraphernalia that would be needed, it was very difficult to clear the aircraft in as tight of a sequence as during early training jumps. And traveling at around 100 mph, a delay of a second or two by any one person resulted in a delay of all that followed. Such accordion patterns weren't all that unforgiving if the DZ was hit, but in the dense hedgerow country of Normandy, this problem was to have disastrous consequences for a great many that jumped that night far from their designated DZ.

So we started jumping out of the back of slow moving trucks onto big open fields at night to determine how fast and efficiently we could assemble. It was sheer nonsense, but we continued to go through that stupid exercise for several nights until somebody began to recognize how ridiculous it was. But without aircraft available for repeated night jumps, I assume the senior officers were willing to try anything in an effort to see what could be done to minimize assembly problems.

Finally, in early May, another night jump was scheduled to determine if some of the mistakes of the previous jump could be corrected. I had been designated the "jump master," and at a routine briefing we were informed that a possible way to improve assembly was to drop the equipment bundles in the middle of the stick instead of immediately ahead of the jump master. To accomplish this new procedure, a white armband was put on the right arm of the machine gun ammo-bearer, who was generally placed in the middle of the stick behind the gunner. The aircraft's crew chief had the responsibility of hitting the bomb-rack toggle switch as the ammo-bearer jumped, thus dropping the equipment bundles at the appropriate time.

We flew around for a couple of hours, then finally the red light flashed on and I ordered, "Stand up and hook up." As we went through the pre-jump routine, the crew chief came back by the open door ready to perform his simple task as we jumped. Peering out into the prop-blast, it was easy to see aircraft to the rear and slightly above, and the aircraft immediately ahead and slightly below. I had never noticed before how much aircraft flying in tight formations moved up, down, and sideways in relation to each other. Suddenly, a green light flashed on in the dome of an aircraft far ahead and, a split second later, our green light flashed on. I hollered, "Let's go!" and jumped out into the blackness.

I landed without incident and almost immediately saw assembly lights in the distance, set up by our pathfinders. We had been dropped right on the money! Then one of my men rushed up to tell me that my ammo-bearer was tangled in the suspension lines of the equipment bundle parachutes, out cold, and bleeding from the mouth. I left one man with him and headed for the assembly area, locating a medic there and sent him back to see what had to be done. As it turned out, the only thing wrong was a huge headache and a cut lip. He was lucky. I was told that some other sticks had serious injuries. That jump was the last time equipment bundles were dumped in the middle of us.

Finally, the day arrived when we boarded the buses and were driven to the Saltby Air Base in the Leicester area of the Midlands. I believe we arrived on June 1st, but it may have been a day or two earlier. Our new home was a huge hanger that formerly housed B-17s. On the outskirts of the largely by-passed airfield were several cannibalized B-17s still sitting where they had been abandoned after serving their final purpose which was supplying some needed parts that would help keep other B-17s flying. On close inspection, it seemed impossible that they could have brought their crews back. Battle damage was clearly visible. I pointed out to whoever would listen that those aircraft getting back home was simply a reflection of the great job I did in building the damn things when I ran the Boeing Company. I think most of my guys wondered why I hadn't stayed there.

Staff Sergeant George H. Menter
Platoon Sergeant

Private First Class Gerald Brightsman

Private Pat Rickard

Sergeant Robert J. Broderick
Squad Leader

18

We had come a long way since Blanding, and now it was time to get on with our job. The thought that we might be left on the sidelines was unthinkable.

For a day or two, we didn't do much of anything. Then on the 3rd of June, the covers came off the "sand tables," maps were issued and we learned that the objective of the 2nd Battalion was to destroy the bridge across the Douve River at Etienville in Normandy. As we studied the sand table, the route from our proposed DZ to the bridge seemed simple enough. All the houses, roads, and obvious landmarks were laid out for us, and Etienville didn't appear to be much of a town to move through. While the entire regiment had specific assigned objectives for each battalion, and each battalion in turn assigned company objectives, my squad of twelve men was simply a part of the overall company's job of assisting and protecting our demolition team as they went about the business of blowing up the bridge. We would then establish defensive positions to protect the southern flank of the American infantry divisions as they proceeded across the Cherbourg Peninsula.

The whole thing sounded rather cut and dried. I did manage to put my foot in my mouth when I suggested that, based on the last couple of night jumps, we probably should have some sort of contingency plan, but Lieutenant Gillespie emphasized that blowing the bridge was our primary objective and that's what we were going to do...period. Later, none of us could remember another time when Gillespie was that angry.

Lieutenant Gillespie, dropped far from the DZ like the rest of us, formed up with others including some "F" Company men, and, determined to carry out his mission, set out in what he assumed was the route to Etienville. Leading the way, he had gone but a short distance when he was cut down by machine gun fire and instantly killed. Sadly, none of us were dropped anywhere near our intended DZ, or that bloody bridge, but our wonderful lieutenant didn't live long enough to learn that. We did develop an unrehearsed contingency plan, however. It was sort of a modern-day version of "Cowboys and Indians" without any indication of just who were the Indians. As many fought for their lives in small groups all over the damn place, I guess we probably were.

All during the 4th of June, the wind howled and the rain came down in torrents. On the 5th, the winds subsided, and the sun came out. Sometime after evening chow, word came down with electrifying news. It was on – we were going!

Within the hour, Brightsman and I picked our parachutes from a big stack, helped each other with fitting the cumbersome things on, and at about 2300 hours (double daylight savings time) moved out to our assigned aircraft.

I cannot remember any of us displaying those stupid "mohawk" haircuts or blackened faces. And I don't remember those "crickets" we were supposed to use for recognition in the darkness; neither do others I've had occasion to talk to. If I had any thoughts at all as I went through the final preparations, it was probably wondering how I had gotten this far without having been tripped up somewhere along the way. I wasn't even apprehensive – I was simply resigned to my fate. Further, I didn't detect anything out of the ordinary among the others. It was almost as though this was to be just another routine night jump, but I suspect that, underneath all of the calm outward appearances, most of us felt much as I did: we had come a long way since Blanding, and now it was time to get on with our job. The thought that we might be left on the sidelines was unthinkable.

I've often wondered what I would have thought had I known that, within the next thirty days, a third of the company would have been killed, and, of the balance, nearly fifty percent would be wearing the Purple Heart, most in hospitals in the States.

Soon after arriving at our aircraft, I went over to Gillespie's and shook hands with him and Joe Harrold, then returned to mine to await the order to "mount up." As the sun was going down, that order arrived and one by one we lumbered up the steps and into the aircraft to take our pre-arranged places on the hard bucket seats that lined both sides. Within minutes, the first engine sprang to life, immediately followed by the second. We slowly taxied out into a line of other aircraft and moved into take-off position. There would be no turning back.

And so we took off into the fading twilight to spearhead the greatest military invasion in the history of the modern world, and my sought-after rendezvous with destiny took on new meaning.

Left to right:
Private Frank McAvoy, Private Cliff Cunningham,
Private Al Ferguson, Private First Class Don Yoon

Left to right: Private Dan Miller,
Private First Class Del Seebach,
Corporal Don Wright

Left to right: Private Ed Vaught,
Private First Class Harry Thompson,
Sergeant Robert J. Broderick

19

To this day, the memory of that night continues to haunt me, for as I jumped out into that maelstrom, I believed I was committing suicide.

The flight into Normandy was boring even though we nearly crashed on take-off. After flying for a couple of hours, we finally crossed the channel into France and started our run toward our drop zone. As we proceeded across the peninsula, it seemed all hell had broken loose. We began getting small arms fire that grew in intensity, and as heavier anti-aircraft fire joined in, I remember the eerie strobe light effect inside the cabin due to the increasingly intense fire being directed at our incoming flights.

Lieutenant Cook gave us the order to stand up and hook up. By now our aircraft was flying through unexpected weather turbulence and the turbulence of exploding anti-aircraft fire.

It swayed and bounced so badly that, loaded down with arms, ammunition, and demolition, it was extremely difficult to maintain our balance while moving toward the door after the green light had flashed on and Cook had yelled, "Let's go!" Even so, the stick went smoothly until suddenly the line stopped with a man down. I turned to Menter and yelled, "Tell the pilot to make another pass." How naïve. Mentor, without unhooking, rushed toward the cockpit only to hear either the pilot or co-pilot scream, "JUMP!" as both engines were already at full throttle and our aircraft was climbing. Presumably, the pilot, feeling his job was done, could think of nothing but just getting the hell out. Meanwhile, the man down, Cliff Cunningham, crawled to the door and tumbled out with the last four of us right behind him into what appeared to be a wall of anti-aircraft fire. To this day, the memory of that night continues to haunt me, for as I jumped out into that maelstrom, I believed I was committing suicide.

As soon as my chute snapped open I seemed to be surrounded by tracers coming up from all directions. As I looked down, I could see their reflection on the water below and, at the same time, knew from experience that we had been dumped too high. I began to climb my risers, pulling my chute almost down in front of me as tracers initially went through my canopy and I slipped rapidly down. Close to the ground, I let go of my risers and slammed into part of the flooded portion near the Merderet River that was not deep enough to drown in, and where there were no Germans covering the area. Because of the relatively deep water and vegetation growing up through it, and I suppose the way that I probably hit the water, I found myself all tangled in my suspension lines. I wouldn't have survived for very long if the Germans had been there.

As I struggled to get out of my harness, (*Those damn snap fasteners*) I continued to watch as serial after serial of incoming aircraft flew through the heavy concentrations of flak. At the time I failed to realize that, because I had had to jump from our high-flying speeding aircraft, at perhaps as much as three times the normal seven hundred feet, I had actually drifted away from most of the flak as I came down. But I was very aware that nobody was shooting at me for the moment.

Even so, I was in an absolute rage. No matter some of the incoming aircraft were on fire, or others with engines screaming, or that the racket was intense, I was so damn mad at the pilot of our aircraft that I would willingly have shot him on sight. In those brief minutes of confusion and anger I thought, *The bastards have done it again*, certain that I had come down a long way from our assigned DZ. And I kept thinking, *What a hell of a way to embark on Eisenhower's Great Crusade*.

In retrospect, instead of being in a rage when I landed in that flooded area, I should have been counting my blessings, for as it turned out, the entire regiment had been mis-dropped, more often than not with tragic consequences. Nobody hit the assigned DZ, but I couldn't know that at the time. The inevitable result was some drowned in the rivers or flooded areas, others landed in the trees to be shot as they dangled helplessly (we were not issued sidearms) while many more landed amongst the Germans to be killed, wounded, or captured trying to get out of those cumbersome parachute harnesses, or soon thereafter in the face of overwhelming odds. But for whatever reason or whatever you believe in, some things turn out to be just dumb luck, or, if you are of a mind, fate, and the hand you are dealt. Fate, it seemed, had intervened for me as it was to do again and again as the days of combat stretched into weeks, then months. Of our sixteen man stick, the first eleven landed on the west side of the Merderet River and the remaining five of us landed on the east side near La Fiere. Thus, the few moments it took for one man to claw his way to the door and tumble out, our high-flying aircraft passed over that damn river.

Many things happen during combat that constitute the fine line between life and death which often seem to defy logic and reasonable explanation. As a survivor of all the campaigns and nearly all the battles with "F" Company, I had my share of encounters with that fine line. But for one man losing his balance at a precise moment in time, five of us would probably have ended up in the middle of the Merderet River and certain death.

20

It was still dark when Menter and some other staff sergeant decided to send a couple of scouts up and down the tracks to. . .hopefully find out where the hell we were.

Free of my harness and with my raging anger subsiding, I sloshed out of the water. Upon reaching dry land, I sat down utterly disgusted, as if I were all alone on the moon. As I began to take stock of my situation, I was suddenly aware that it had become very quiet. No more aircraft flying overhead and the pounding of the flak batteries had stopped. As my eyes grew accustomed to the dark, I noticed what appeared to be a roadbed at the top of a nearby embankment. I assumed it must be the road leading to Etienville. At the same time, I began looking for the assembly lights our pathfinders were to set up, and wondering where Menter and the others were. All the time thinking I couldn't be very far from the DZ, I climbed the bank and was stunned to find not a road, but railroad tracks instead, and I knew then that I had not only missed the target, but missed it by a lot. But that was all I knew. While I had viewed the railroad line running south from Cherbourg during our pre-Normandy briefing, it never dawned on me that any of us would end up astride it. I knew I could be anywhere from Cherbourg to Carentan. About this time, I began to hear sporadic shots, so I thought to myself, *When in doubt, head for the sound of gunfire.* I started down the tracks and ran into Menter, and a short time later, Cunningham, Yoon, and several others that had also come down in the flood waters of the Merderet. Everyone was soaking wet and most were as pissed off as I was.

Incredibly, nobody was shooting at us even though we were pretty good targets as we stood around trying to figure out what to do next. It was still dark when Menter and some other Staff Sergeant decided to send a couple of scouts up and down the tracks to see if they could locate friend or foe, and hopefully find out where the hell we were.

It was starting to get light when one of the scouts returned to say he had encountered some other paratroopers who thought the firing we were hearing from time to time was coming from Chef-du-Pont and some action developing at a farm complex that Germans were defending. At this time, we had already moved from where we had landed, and as we were not under any direct fire, we blundered along atop the railroad embankment, seemingly oblivious to danger. It was as though we were taking a stroll in Central Park. As it turned out, we were some distance from the Chef-du-Pont and the place we were heading for was named La Fiere, its causeway, and the small bridge across the Merderet, none of which were shown on our maps.

The subsequent fight for the La Fiere causeway developed into one of the most murderous actions in all of Normandy, but as we shall see, our little group did not participate, even though we were there initially.

I should note that, before the week was over, we became acutely aware of the difference between our machine guns and the "Tommy" gun, and the German counterparts. There actually was no comparison. We had nothing that could compare with the German MG 42 or their machine pistol, the deadly Schmeisser, both with a much greater cyclic rate of fire, so much so that at times the sound of their machine guns produced their own echo. Until you knew better, it sounded like a deadly duet. A Schmeisser, firing directly in front of you sounded much like ripping canvas. If you survived, it was something you would never forget.

At some point, we moved away from the railroad tracks, crossed some small fields, and arrived at the first in a series of farm buildings. We passed a dead paratrooper (sadly, there would be several more) that apparently had been among the first to confront the Germans during the predawn darkness.

A short distance further loomed the Manoir at La Fiere, and there we took up positions along the high ground to the rear of the building and began firing into the windowless aperture on the second floor (main level) just to keep the German's heads down. Meanwhile, Menter, intent on carrying out Lieutenant Gillespie's admonishment that, "The bridge at Eteinville was our objective," left to find some other rout as the bridge and the causeway were already blocked by the Germans. So the whole morning was now slipping by as we cooled our heels figuring that at any moment we'd be on our way to Eteinville, and although a little bit late, lend our support in accomplishing our company's assignment.

The Manoir was actually a local farmer's house that, because of its close proximity to the causeway and the small bridge over the Merderet River, had been taken over by the Germans. It was a two-story affair that was almost fortress-like because of its stone walls. There were several structures attached to, or in close proximity to, the main building. Situated a short distance from the river, it initially received a lot of attention because the Germans had elected to defend it. The real action, however, was developing on the causeway, and that was attracting a hoard of paratroopers, like us, dumped far from their intended DZ, and looking for any kind of a fight amid all the confusion.

The Merderet River normally was little more than a centuries-old meandering stream that had taken on a very different character after the Germans, as a defense measure, flooded the entire area some months prior to the invasion.

Thus the little Merderet had disappeared under a sea of water and only the causeway and the bridge were now visible, the former assumed tremendous tactical importance, all out of proportion to its size.

Actually, from our position during the early hours, there didn't seem to be much going on the at causeway itself. We had been told that a group of paratroopers had already crossed it, but apparently had simply moved on. Unfortunately, nobody had thought to secure the area across from La Fiere. As a result, within a very short time, the Germans arrived in force and took control of that end of the causeway, thereby denying the Americans a vital route east for several days. It was a major blunder. During that time, one of the bloodiest small battles in all of Normandy raged, and it was our glider infantrymen that took the brunt of it. But even though it was obvious to some of us that the fight for control of the causeway was increasing in intensity, we continued with our task of trying to get the Germans in the Manoir to surrender. Meanwhile, a growing number of paratroopers, all complete strangers, would arrive on the scene, ask a few questions, take a few pot shots at the damned place, and then move on.

The Manoir House
Photo Taken in 1997

21

The fight for the Manoir was never any big deal.
Reading some accounts now appearing in print are,
for the most part, pure fiction.

With Menter gone, we weren't at all interested in joining the growing number of paratroopers milling around the causeway. For all we knew, that bunch was trying to accomplish their objective. We sure as hell weren't doing a thing to help accomplish ours. Funny enough, I remember thinking that Gillespie would chew us out for not getting to Eteinville on time, but what the hell, Menter was in charge. We would have been shocked if we had known "F" Company didn't even exist as a fighting unit and nobody in the company ever got near that bridge across the Douve River. Maybe it was just as well that we were poorly dropped, for apparently, Eteinville was crawling with Germans.

The fight for the Manoir was never any big deal. Reading some accounts now appearing in print are, for the most part, pure fiction. Actually, those of us trying to dislodge the Germans were stymied until some guy showed up with a Bazooka and managed to put a round through one of the apertures. The results were immediate and devastating and the white surrender flags began appearing.

While it was obvious by now that activity down on the causeway was turning into a very significant battle, there seemed to be a lessening of the confusion that had prevailed earlier at the Manoir, particularly when Colonel Lindquist and several other officers made their appearance. To say that I was surprised to see him is an understatement. My thought was, *What the hell is he doing here? We're nowhere near the DZ.* Then some officer spotted my sergeant stripes and told me to round up some men and have them remove the dead and wounded from inside the Manoir so that the French family could reoccupy their home. The only privates I recognized were Cliff and Don, so I told them what I wanted done.

The next thing I knew, a body came flying out of an upper level window and landed with a thud in the courtyard where a few of us were standing. Before anyone could say a word, a second body came flying out in much that same fashion to land beside the first body. Then Don leaned out the window, spit down in the direction of the fallen enemy and then smiled at me as if to say, *How's that, Sergeant?* But, while some of us laughed, the same officer that had told me to remove the Germans now hastily instructed me to find a more dignified way of handling the problem.

Unfortunately, Don was killed a couple of weeks later, while Cliff, unable to continue due to deteriorating health, was hospitalized, then sent home and given a medical discharge.

I don't have any idea what happened to the prisoners. Although we had been ordered not to take any prisoners, with few exceptions that order was never carried out. Generally, prisoners were not mistreated, at least not that I was aware of, and enemy wounded did receive medical attention.

I remember quite clearly when one German was brought out of the Manoir and placed, sitting up, against a wall. He appeared to be middle-aged, a private, his entire lower body perforated with fatal wounds. He was obviously near death, and the expression on his face was one that I was to see in others that suffered such injuries but somehow still remained semi-conscious. It was a look of confusion and/or bewilderment, usually without fear as their lives slipped away. This was the first time I had watched a man die. Later that afternoon, I stopped to try and say a word or two with an old friend from our days at Blanding. He had been shot in the stomach, but was too far gone to recognize me. He died a short time later.

Sometime following the surrender of the Germans at the Manoir, while we were waiting for Menter to return, out of boredom and curiosity, I decided to venture down to the causeway to see what the increasing racket was all about. For a short time I watched our artillerymen roll up a 57MM that had come in by glider during the night, and, although totally exposed to enemy fire, began shooting at the German tanks now on the causeway and moving toward our side. At almost point-blank range, the lead tank was stopped, thereby blocking the narrow roadway and preventing other tanks from crossing. Unfortunately, I believe the entire artillery crew was killed a short time later. It was an incredible sight as I stood there gawking like a spectator at a sporting event. With the Germans rapidly building up substantial strength, it's amazing that I hadn't been pressed into that desperate battle – probably because there were so many other paratroopers milling about. In any event, I thought, *To hell with it*, and went back to the Manoir.

22

An infantryman is always a bit nervous when he can't get below ground, but there was nothing we could do.

I can't remember whether Menter had returned or not, but it turned out we weren't going anywhere, certainly not to Etienville: for about this time Joe Harrold, Glen Bell, and Ed Vaught arrived at the Manoir, soaking wet, having waded and swam across the Merderet and surrounding inundated area, under intense enemy fire. Lieutenant Snee had been with them but had been killed at some point during the crossing. Snee had been a replacement that joined us while we were in Ireland.

As we compared notes with the new arrivals, it started to dawn on us that something had gone very wrong. Although both Joe and Glen had jumped with Gillespie, neither had seen him, or any of the others in their stick once on the ground.

While we were talking, some officer came and asked what

regiment we were from, and when we responded 508, he told us to join others from the 508, move back to the railroad tracks, set up a defensive position so as to guard the rear of the Manoir and the all-important causeway. We didn't realize it at the time, but he, in effect, was ordering us away from the murderous fight for control of the causeway that was increasing in intensity hour by hour.

I can only speculate as to why we were so fortunate. The answer probably was recognition that the rear of the paratrooper's position was vulnerable, and the rag-tag bunch of 508'ers would form at least some sort of cohesive force, as the majority of those paratroopers engaged on and around the causeway were from other regiments. Those officers that had finally taken some measure of control over what had been a rather chaotic situation realized that the best way to do that was to put the guys under their own officers and/or NCO's that were on the scene.

But that's just speculation. I do know that most of us learned early on that, in combat situations, junior officers and sergeants could rarely give orders to, nor control, paratroopers from different outfits, or from their own outfit if they didn't know the guys they were dealing with. The Germans had no such problems.

It was probably late afternoon by the time we arrived at the general area where we were to set up defensive positions. I spread my four men along a tree line and then began digging in immediately above the tracks and adjacent to a cattle bridge that spanned them. In just moments, it became obvious that we couldn't dig in. The trees were ancient and had formidable root systems that defied our shovels. And for eons, cattle had trampled the soil into concrete. An infantryman is always a bit nervous when he can't get below ground, but there was nothing we could do. We couldn't abandon the area, so we just waited for a possible German attack. But we were not prepared for what was to follow.

The rocket fire that descended on us as we lay atop the ground was awesome. This was our first introduction to the multi-rocket "screaming meemies." Being under artillery barrage was terrifying enough, but unless you've been exposed to a rocket attack, you simply cannot imagine what it's like. The shriek of those incoming rockets initially created a sound, and terror, unmatched by anything any of us had heard before. Months later we were under repeated rocket attacks in Holland, but got used to them. The fireball coming in on us was easy to follow, unlike the artillery and mortar shells, and the sound became just a nuisance. In any event, the attack didn't last very long and, as far as I know, only got one man, Ed Vaught. He survived, actually, but never returned to the company. As quickly as it had begun, the rocket barrage stopped. To our amazement, the sky filled with C-47s towing the glider infantry, and the Germans turned their attention to them.

The landings of those flimsy gliders were, more often than not, tragic. From my position, I did not see any of them find the ground as the hedgerows and trees blocked my view, but on patrol the following morning, I passed several that had crashed. The bodies of unfortunate glider infantrymen spread all around the scene told its own story. I relieved a couple of clips for my 45 from the body of a pilot who had flown into one of those damn hedgerows, which was virtually a stone wall to a flimsy glider.

After Normandy, paratroopers stopped looking down their noses at glidermen. Not ever again.

23

Hunger, fatigue, fear, and even boredom were
our constant companions.

At dawn on the 7th of June, some officers came by, and one told me to come with him. I didn't know who the hell he was, however, he was about to lead a patrol out and apparently wanted a sergeant to bring up the rear. I told Cliff (or Don) to inform Menter, and I followed this officer as the group formed up.

The patrol consisted of about a dozen men, all complete strangers. Side note: in January, 1997, by a strange set of circumstances, one of the guys that had been on that patrol that day phoned me on another matter and we started comparing notes... What a small world. Anyway, we moved out from our position near the railroad tracks without any instructions or comments from the officer leading, and for several hours moved from one small field to another. The hedgerows were often so thick, I didn't have a clue where the hell we were or where the hell we were going. "Sergeant, you bring up the rear" – big damn deal. Here I was, deep in enemy territory on patrol, led by an officer I didn't know and in the company of guys I'd never seen before. I couldn't help but wonder what I was doing there when I should be with the guys trying to get to our objective.

During the patrol, we came under some minor enemy small-arms fire and proceeded to return it, targeting a small farmhouse. But the Germans, apparently, had no interest in defending the place and simply melted away. We had one guy slightly wounded. After a brief inspection, it became obvious that the Germans were just scrounging for food. We then continued to move around for the balance of the early afternoon. From time to time we would just do nothing. I don't remember ever talking to any of the others on that patrol, certainly not the guy leading it.

Actually, I was furious. I was certain people all over Normandy were engaged in accomplishing their assigned objectives, not withstanding some doubts after seeing Colonel Lindquist the morning before, far from his objective. Here I was, out tramping around the Norman countryside like a Boy Scout, and except for that brief encounter at the farmhouse, there was not a single shot fired by "thems" or us. While it certainly was no game we were playing, the truth is that it was just plain boring. Imagine it, I spent my second day on the ground, deep in enemy territory, bored to death.

Later on, after giving it some thought, I finally concluded that our patrol must have been just one of many, each sent out to cover a specific area, and that the officer leading our patrol pretty much knew what he was about. Some patrols, like ours, didn't amount to much, while others simply failed to return. By the time I'd spent months in combat, I became very familiar with patrol activity and realized how dangerous it was. Ultimately, it scared the hell out of me. But from my first one, I'd never have known.

I have absolutely no recollection of returning to La Fiere area or what time of day it might have been. I simply rejoined Menter and the others. I can't even remember asking them what they had been doing all day. But it was obvious that none of us had run into any serious opposition from the Germans. Most of the available ones on our side of the Merderet were undoubtedly engaged in the fighting in and around St. Mere Eglise, hence the area between there and La Fiere was not defended to any extent.

Events between the 8th and the 12th of June are beyond recall. While there was a lot going on, I can't put the pieces together in any coherent way. Hunger, fatigue, fear, and even boredom were our constant companions. Somebody once said that combat is fifty-nine minutes of boredom and sixty seconds of stark terror, and that is pretty close to the truth.

Although, at times, the reverse was also true. The actual encounters with the Germans were infrequent, almost always brief, often violent, and absolutely confusing in that jungle-like hedgerow country where we were fighting.

All of us that survived learned early on some pretty fundamental ways to keep on living. It was one thing to attack against rifle fire, quite another to confront a machine gun. Getting hit by artillery or mortar fire was just a roll of the dice. Especially the latter. Of all the weapons we faced, mortar fire was the most indiscriminate, silent in trajectory and devastating upon impact.

I do remember once, when confronted by bullets from a machine gun, and discretion being the better part of valor, hitting the ground and crawling out of the line of fire. One way or another, we'd get in position to attack. It was a heart-thumping business. On one such occasion, after we had taken care of the Germans, I discovered I had a hell of a nosebleed. One of the guys asked me if I had been hit and I replied, "No, but my blood pressure must have gotten a bit high."

For all the life-threatening encounters and combat days against the enemy, I believe I survived simply because, for whatever reason, I always seemed to be in the "eye of the hurricane." Perhaps, as some have suggested, I had a very special guardian angel, but I personally consider such stuff little more than superstition.

24

We were supposed to be among the most highly trained troops in the world. We weren't, but something must have worked because we always got the job done.

During and/or after an encounter with the enemy, the dead and wounded, both theirs and ours, were generally ignored. We didn't want to know and often didn't care. If a casualty was one of your own men, you reported the status. It was enough to know that the medics would take care of the wounded. The dead didn't matter. Although the death of Brightsman was personally devastating, none of us could let casualties get to us, or we could no longer function.

Over the long months of training, I can remember only one or two times that we had the opportunity to fire live ammunition. Of course, we had no way of knowing that ammunition was in critical supply during that period. We were supposed to be among the most highly trained troops in the world. We weren't, but something must have worked because we always got the job done. What we had was a lot of WWI infantry techniques, useless in Normandy. Fire fights developed rapidly and events often moved so fast that there was not time to think about anything except to fire at whoever came into view, and most of the time "from the hip." If you took the time to aim carefully, you'd be dead before you could pull the trigger. Most of the time, I'm sure I missed whomever I was shooting at. A few times I knew I hadn't. Killing was what the damn infantry was all about. Oddly, most of us accepted that with incredible indifference. There were a few that seemed to enjoy the killing, but to most of us it was just some horrible experience that went with our job.

I believe we arrived in the town of Chef-du-Pont during the afternoon of the 8th. The officer that had led us from the La Fiere area disappeared, leaving Menter in command of our rag-tag group. I can't recall where Joe Harrold or Glen Bell were at the time. There was obviously a great deal of activity going on in and around the town, and on out to the Chef-du-Pont causeway and bridge. As with the protracted fight for control of the La Fiere causeway, another battle was in progress at our present location. But we were mixed in with a ton of other paratroopers and none of us knew what the hell we were doing there, all of which increased our frustration and concern.

By then, it was almost like we were AWOL. We didn't seem to

be getting any closer to rejoining the company that we had been on D-Day. We just seemed to be drifting from one place to another. We had had some brief encounters with the Germans earlier, but nothing that amounted to anything of importance. Just hit-and-miss stuff that had little meaning other than another delay in getting to where we wanted to go.

Our arrival in Chef-du-Pont soon put our concerns to rest. It became quite clear that we weren't going anywhere from this place either, at least not for the time being.

As we came into the town, we stopped briefly near a railroad siding to watch the antics of a bunch of paratroopers blowing open the door of a French "40 et 8" boxcar. While a couple of them proceeded to roll out some cheese wheels, others amused themselves throwing French paper money into the air to be scattered by the wind down the dusty street. That paper money was the German payroll for the troops in our area. We just laughed, not realizing it was genuine currency and that same currency would be our payroll in a few months. The cheese was absolutely delicious, and as we were starving, we stuffed ourselves on it. As necessity is the mother of invention, using the larger French francs, about $20.00, as toilet paper provided a bit of comfort, especially for those of us who had landed in water, destroying our original supply.

In and around Chef-du-Pont were a lot of brave and eager young Frenchmen, all sporting orange arm-bands and carrying whatever weapons they could get their hands on, and all trying to help out. Unfortunately, they were not allowed to fight alongside our troops.

Moving Up
June, 1944

25

The hedgerows were so thick at times that I never saw a German, but as bullets ripped the foliage around and above us, we knew they were never far away.

We had strolled down toward the river when some officer with about a dozen paratroopers in tow came up to Menter and me and, with a sweep of his arm, told us to set up a defensive position facing the river. Aside from Cliff and Don, I didn't know any of the new arrivals. Menter left me in charge and I spread the guys along a hedgerow and told them to dig in. I don't know where Menter had disappeared to, but while we could clearly hear the sound of battle coming from the vicinity of the causeway a short distance from us, we could just as well have been in London. It was another boring assignment and we promptly fell asleep. When I awoke with the sunrise, all the guys but Cliff and Don began drifting away to find something more interesting to do. When the officer came back a few hours later, he asked me if I had had any problems during the night. I remember telling him things were pretty quiet, and hoping to hell he wouldn't ask me where all the guys were that were supposed to be defending our little patch of Normandy.

No matter. Soon thereafter, Menter showed up and we moved down to where the sound of the continuing battle for possession of that vital causeway was now very close by. And, as at La Fiere, there seemed to be a large number of paratroopers on the scene, some just milling about. We settled down a short distance away from the action to await further orders, during which, we were alerted several times and told to be ready to move out at a moment's notice. But for whatever reason, the order came only once, late at night, and ended in what seemed to be total confusion. At any rate, we spent the night a few hundred yards from the causeway and for all practical purposes, out of harm's way.

At dawn, Menter rounded us up and with some other paratroopers moved out in what we all presumed to be a sweep to clear any Germans from the area. So began another one of those minor, brief encounters with the enemy: a lot of sporadic firing on both sides, without a clue what the results were, except that we kept moving from one field to another. The hedgerows were so thick at times that I never saw a German, but as bullets ripped the foliage around and above us, we knew they were never far away.

The whole thing was one of slow frustrating progress, impossible to control and never really knowing who was where...them or us. I remember we had generally advanced with a road in view but often became disoriented, working our way through that "jungle." Any attempt to abandon the protection of the hedgerow, and move out onto the road or the open fields, was a sure way to get killed.

Somewhere along the way we lost contact with the other paratroopers we had started out with, and, as the Germans made no real problems for us at the time, our usual procedure was to simply say, "To hell with it," and take a break. Menter and I were just resting against one of the hedgerows, dog-tired, hungry, filthy dirty, and running low on ammunition, when we recognized we were up against a relatively small group of Germans employing delay tactics that they were very good at in what had become their "home territory." And it was pretty obvious to us that the Germans were not attempting any real defense of this turf even though we had kept up the pressure as we continued to push them out of one field after another.

26

He had what he remembered as a "certain feeling of fatalism. There is nothing you can do about it. You become oblivious to the deaths and wounds all around. You become a detached person, viewing it from a distance, even though it is going on right at your feet."
Tom Brokaw, The Greatest Generation,
Quoting Senator Mark Hatfield

It was about this time when we heard the approach of what sounded like a tracked vehicle. It turned out to be a US Army "weasel," a small weapons carrier and the first one we had ever seen, with a young infantry 2nd lieutenant sitting in it and surrounded by his platoon. Their sergeant appeared to be an older guy, probably in his thirties. From time to time, long-range artillery would roar overhead, obviously coming from the beach area, seeking targets farther inland and certainly of no threat to us. With each salvo, the entire platoon, except the sergeant, would crouch down or go to the ground. It didn't matter to most of them when told it was our artillery. At any rate, we briefed the lieutenant on what we had been encountering for most of the morning and we both tried to convince him to get out of the vehicle, get his men off the road, and continue his advance on the edge of the hedgerow or the adjacent fields that offered at least some cover. He rejected our advice, probably thinking we just wanted to acquire his little vehicle. And so he and his cautious platoon proceeded up the road. Sadly, heavy machine gun fire told us they didn't get very far. And we really didn't care.

The infantry was passing through us. No wonder the Germans hadn't put up much of a fight, offering only token resistance. They probably were more aware of the advancing American Infantry than we were.

At some point we returned to the vicinity of the La Fiere causeway. Stepping over and around the American and German dead and mangled bodies that littered the entire area, we crossed over the causeway on our way to Hill 30 where the far-flung remnants of our 2nd Battalion were in the process of assembling. During the passage, we moved through some small villages to spend time amongst the dead, identifying several of our own F Company men still laying where they had fallen. Again, the dead were all over the place, but for some reason they didn't seem to matter to me. I had already shut everything out of my mind, except for the moment.

After an hour or so, we continued on our way, arriving on Hill 30 during the late afternoon of June 11th. So while Menter, Cunningham, Yoon and I had been engaged in relatively minor skirmishes since D-Day, we had somehow been spared involvement in the countless battles so murderous that those who inexplicably were drawn into them paid with their lives.

Those of us still breathing could look forward to being relieved, and felt we would soon be back in Nottingham to those lovely ladies, the booze, and time enough to enjoy life again before our next rendezvous with death.

How wrong we were...

27

We became vaguely aware that the whole airborne drop had been a disaster; what historians would later describe as done with almost criminal negligence.

The causeways at La Fiere and the Chef-du-Pont were now secure. On the afternoon of the 11th of June we crossed over the La Fiere causeway to join, for the first time since we jumped, what remained of the 2nd Battalion that had been engaged in the bitter fighting around Hill 30. The causeway was absolutely littered with the dead, both theirs and ours. We had some joyous reunions with those of our company who we were seeing for the first time since the drop. Brightsman gave me a bear-hug that nearly killed me, while more than one expressed amazement at seeing me as the word had circulated that I had been killed. Everybody had a story to tell, the savage in-fighting sort of, "Can you top this?" And while the Germans were still only a few hundred yards away, nothing seemed to dampen our spirits.

Reality was something else, however. Of our once proud company of nine officers and one hundred twenty EM's, only three officers and approximately forty EM's were present and accounted for. Lieutenant Gillespie was dead and Lieutenant Cook would die on July 4th. I never saw either of them again. At that time, we had no knowledge of what had happened to the rest of the company. We became vaguely aware that the whole airborne drop had been a disaster; what historians would later describe as done with almost criminal negligence. Certainly the pilot of my aircraft acted in a cowardly manner.

I can't remember who was there at that date. I really didn't pay much attention to anyone other than my own men. I do recall some of those that were present to attack across the Douve River the night of June 12th in whatever would float, some of us using our rifles as paddles. We had been resupplied with ammunition and rations during the day and now we were to attack the town of Beuzeville la Bastille and secure the area while engineers put a Baily Bridge over the river. Menter was there; Brightsman, Cunningham, and Yoon were all that remained of my squad. Joe Harrold was there with Bell, Elash, Campbell, and a couple of others from his squad. Ward and Snapp were there as well as Kulwicki, Lokan, Niemic, and Kincaid. Sadly, they were to die later on that day. And others, of course. Fraser, Polette, and Goodale were the only officers, but Fraser panicked when a tank opened fire on us as we reached the other side of the river, so he and McKee swam back across it. Colonel Shanley relieved Fraser on the spot. Actually, the tank was small, lightly armed and quickly disposed of. I heard that tank coming down the road and headed in its direction, only to be knocked over backward by a terrific explosion, blowing a grenade and my first-aid packet off my harness. My first thought as I got back on my feet was that the tank had opened fire at point-blank range and missed me. It wasn't until I was back with the company talking with Polette that he told me that Bill Snapp had reached the tank first and threw a Gammon with two sticks of C-2 stuffed in the sock. It's no wonder the explosion had knocked me down, a single stick of C-2 would have been enough to kill the Germans. Two sticks was absolutely devastating. At this point, there was supposed to be artillery barrage laid down on the town to soften up the Germans prior to our attack, but for whatever reason, it failed to materialize.

We moved out toward the town, Joe Harrold on the left side of the road and me on the right side, and as we led the company down through the town of Beuzeville la Bastille, I remember thinking how easy it would have been for the Germans to ambush us. Anyone familiar with small European towns knows that the building fronting the roads formed effective walls offering absolutely no cover. But the Germans had fled and the town appeared deserted. The engineers put the Bailey Bridge across the Douve, the battalion crossed over at dawn, and we then joined them for the long march toward Baupte, the next town we were to attack.

There were a couple interruptions along the way, quickly disposed of. Tank-riding Germans came down the road to attack us. The lead company killed all fifteen or twenty young Germans that some fool had sent out thinking, I suppose, that they and their small tanks could stop us.

I can't remember why "F" Company found itself in the lead again as we approached Baupte, but we were, and we walked into a 20mm Flak battery that opened fire as we got into range. Lokan, Kincaid, and Niemic were killed about that time. We then received word from the battalion to hold up as we had gotten out ahead of the other companies. We stayed on the road; the other companies had been fighting minor skirmishes on the flanks. So we settled down behind some hedgerows a short distance from the Germans and just laid around and let the Germans waste a lot of ammunition firing at everything that moved.

Polette had handed me his canteen filled with Calvados, a brandy from Normandy, and I took a big swig that nearly floored me. It had been raining off and on, so after the initial shock, the drink felt good. The Germans seemed far, far away and I was getting drowsy as it had been twenty-four hours since we had had any sleep. But I should have attended to my rifle. At times I could fire entire clips without any noticeable malfunctions, but at other times, my rifle would simply jam open and I'd have to ram the bolt home manually. But I hadn't had any occasion to fire at anything during the last twenty-four hours, so I just ignored the problem. What I should have done was throw the damn thing away and pick up another when I had the chance. There were lots of M-1s laying around in some of the places we'd fought over during the past few days. But I didn't. And because I didn't, my own negligence may have saved my life.

After a half-hour or so, the order came to attack, which we immediately did. Menter led some of us down through a couple of small fields, turned South and came out on the road occupied by the Germans who, at the time, were so intent on firing where we had been, that they failed to see us coming. As I was now in the lead, I shot the closest German and my rifle jammed open again. The rest of them, taken completely by surprise, abandoned their guns and started running with everybody now firing. Ward had jumped up on a tree stump and, totally exposed, was shooting at them with vigor. I had just ordered him to get down and at the same time was reaching for the graphite in the stock of my rifle when suddenly my head seemed to explode. Ward later told me I simply said, "I'm hit," and sat down.

28

As darkness approached, we ended up at a front-line M-A-S-H hospital, and my brief combat time in Normandy ended after just eight days.

I had not the faintest notion where I'd been hit, but do remember looking at my hands and feet. Almost immediately, Lieutenant Polette came running up and asked me who my assistant was. I told him I no longer had one, so he started yelling for Glen Bell. Moments later, he followed Kulwicki through an opening in the hedgerow and Kulwicki was shot dead. Polette told me later, back at Wollaton Park, that he had then killed the German who had shot me and Kulwicki. Don Haupe, a medic, arrived and began putting a bandage around my neck as I was bleeding badly. The attack swept on toward Baupte. Haupe left and I found myself alone with some of our dead and some of theirs.

It wasn't very long before I began to realize that I wasn't hurt very badly, suffering just a massive headache, and having considerable difficulty moving my head without a lot of pain, so I decided to walk to Baupte. About that time a Jeep came along, traveling to the same destination. The driver said the battalion had told him we had taken Baupte, including a bunch of prisoners, that he would be right back and that I should wait for him. After what seemed like an eternity, he came back carrying that crazy Lt. Bolger (E Company officer) on a stretcher mounted crossways over the back seat. Bolger had been shot in the back, and although in considerable pain, complained that one of his own men must have shot him. Alas, eyewitnesses later told me that a German had in fact shot him. I had learned long ago that Bolger was a contemptible son-of-a-bitch. So, armed with the driver's Thompson, as I had no further use for my M-1, I rode shotgun back along the same road we had come up that morning, past the dead Germans along the road that was still a no-man's land. But it was an uneventful ride, albeit quite painful for both Bolger and me. As darkness approached, we ended up at a front-line M-A-S-H hospital and my brief combat time in Normandy ended after just eight days.

I was what was known as walking-wounded, slightly inured in action, hence walked into the hospital on my own power, but was immediately instructed to lie down on one of the available cots. By this time, I was in considerable pain and could not move my head at all. In order to lie down, I had to cup my hands behind my head to support it because gravity was working against me. It was days before I was able to move it with any amount of freedom. And the hell of it was, the wound was little more than a scratch. But I certainly was of no further use to my company during the following month.

Soon, a nurse came and began relieving me of what ammunition and grenades I still carried. But when it came to the Gammon grenade, I refused to allow her to take it, or even touch it. As forcefully as I could, I told her that improper handling of it could blow up most of the hospital. I really think I frightened her as she quickly left, only to return with a doctor. I explained to the doctor how a Gammon functioned and if left lying around, some curious person could very easily set it off. I recommended he get it into the hands of a paratrooper or combat engineer, both familiar with C-2. The doctor thanked me for my concern and assured me he would follow my advice and instructions, so I surrendered the Gammon to him.

Sometime later in the night I was walked to an operating tent. A chaplain offered me some hot food, probably C-rations, and together with some other wounded, just sat on the bare ground and watched the doctors and nurses go about the business of trying to save the more seriously wounded. Unlike the TV show, the real M-A-S-H operating room was simply a tent... very small, quiet, and orderly. Finally, during the early hours of June 14th, I was on the operating table. I can still remember the doctor gently taping my exposed spine and saying, "Sergeant, you are the luckiest son-of-a-bitch I've seen since I hit the beach". Then they did what was required, including a drain tube in my neck, and when they had finished, I was carried to a recovery tent where, for the first time in ten days, I slept like a baby.

On the morning of June 14th, I was taken down to the beachhead. What a sight! Men, equipment, and ships as far as the eye could see. I was given a tetanus booster shot that was more painful than the bullet wound. But, what the hell, everybody was very nice to me. I was treated like royalty in spite of stinking to high heaven, without a shower in two weeks, in a filthy, gas-impregnated, blood-soaked jump suit.

Late in the afternoon, I walked down to the shore, climbed aboard a DUKW, a sea-going truck, with other wounded to be ferried out to the LST 508. What a strange coincidence to board a ship having the same numerical designation as my regiment. The ship was packed with the wounded lying on stretchers that covered the entire floor and the sidewalls. However, no critically wounded were evacuated in this manner. That night, German bombers flew over the beachhead and every damned gun ashore and on the ships at sea opened fire. The racket was unbelievable and some of the wounded began to panic as at least one bomb landed close enough to rock the ship. There was an infantry lieutenant above me on a sidewall stretcher, his head completely swathed in bloody bandages. At the height of the bombing, I told the poor guy that in the event we were hit, I would personally carry him out. He nodded his head that he understood. It was just BS on my part, there was absolutely no way out of that ship if it took a major hit, but it took my mind off the racket and may have given the lieutenant some comfort. But as quickly as it had begun, the firing stopped, and I finally laid down and went to sleep.

The following morning, I went up on deck and there, off in the distance, were the White Cliffs of Dover. Again, I was treated like royalty. I had breakfast in the galley consisting of real white bread, eggs, coffee, and sailors asking all kinds of questions. Some even wanted to shake my hand or just talk. I suppose it was because none of them had ever seen a paratrooper before, and I was just a curiosity.

1st Lt. Lloyd L. Polette
Distinguished Service Cross
Silver Star / Oak Leaf Cluster
Killed in Action, January, 1945

29

...fleeting memories of many of those days, that even after all this time continue to slip in and out of my mind like some haunting nightmare that will not go away.

I don't exactly know where we finally landed, but it was somewhere in southern England. It had been a beautiful crossing. Warm blue skies and a calm sea. The LST let down the ramp and I walked off the ship to waiting ambulances. They took us to a hospital train that had all the windows shuttered. We could see out but the English couldn't see in, bad for civilian morale and all that rot. Some hours later we arrived at a general hospital where I was to lay around for the next couple of weeks. The only problem I had was bringing my 45 into the hospital and putting it under my pillow. Hell, I didn't know the nurses changed the sheets every day! I hadn't seen a bed sheet in months! Nor did I know that bringing a gun into a hospital was simply not allowed. But a major was very nice about it and returned my gun to me when I was discharged. And several of the senior officers wanted to buy my jump boots. I don't know what they did with my bloody, filthy, jump suit. It disappeared, and I was issued a regulation Class "A" uniform as a replacement. Normandy was the last time paratroopers were outfitted in the exclusive and beloved tan jumpsuits.

The formal awarding of the Purple Heart was quite a surprise. About ten of us were lined up, some in pajamas, on the parade grounds. The band started playing and the hospital personnel, dressed in their finest Class "A" uniforms, passed in review. I almost burst out laughing as the nurses marched by, for as an infantryman, I had never seen women march before. Then the colonel commanding the hospital came down the line and pinned the Purple Heart on each of us in turn. For the entire staff of the hospital, we were the first casualties coming out of Normandy and probably the first battle casualties they had ever seen. I suppose they considered us as heroes of some sort.

I think I may have disappointed the little ward doctor who elected to walk back with me following the ceremony, for I had removed the medal from my jacket and put it in my pocket. He couldn't understand why I didn't leave it on for all the world to see. But I couldn't explain how I felt about such nonsense. Getting a Purple Heart meant you weren't with your men doing what you were paid to do. There was a lot of pride in being a paratrooper and laying around at some base hospital for a slight wound didn't seem right at the time. As the months of combat dragged on, there were many times when another such Purple Heart would have looked pretty good to me. As we continued our walk back to the ward, I remember suggesting somewhat in jest, that the paratroops were always looking for volunteers, including doctors. He could then probably get his own Purple Heart. I don't recall his response.

After I was discharged from the hospital, I was sent through the Army's relocation center. In this case it was the infamous center at Litchfield where life for the regular infantryman was made as unbearable as possible in order to get them back into combat. But Paratroopers and Rangers were billeted far across the parade grounds from all the other troops and absolutely left alone for the day or two it took to process the paperwork and issue new travel orders. The MP's that ran the place rarely came near us. A team of psychiatrists interviewed all of the paratroopers and rangers with questions regarding death, fear, nightmares, and the prospect of returning to combat. I seem to recall that one of them off-handedly remarked that it was quite different talking to us than talking to regular infantrymen vis-à-vis attitude, spirit, and morale.

In any event, I soon found myself on a train back to Nottingham, arriving at camp about a week ahead of what was left of the company.

Nothing was ever the same again...

Here, my brief combat narrative must end.

I am well aware that some of my loved ones would like me to continue on into those long, tedious months that followed Normandy: in Holland, Belgium, and Germany. But I am afraid such a task will just keep me awake nights, staring at the ceiling. Recalling Normandy was difficult enough, but I had long ago realized that I simply could not bring myself to write about the sheer horror of battle, nor what it was really like to live like an animal in that savage world of the combat infantryman.

It is one thing to often reflect briefly on the war and talk in generalities about wartime experiences, but it is quite another matter to put into writing fleeting memories of many of those days, that even after all this time continue to slip in and out of my mind like some haunting nightmare that will not go away.

How on earth can I describe what it was like to repeatedly face German machine guns or the nerve-racking shriek of incoming artillery and rocket fire that constantly rained down on our positions. The death and terrible wounds that always followed are beyond description. To try and explain what it was like to shoot another human being, often young soldiers like ourselves, and then carry on as though just being alive for the moment was justification enough, is impossible.

Most of the time I was just doing my job and attempting to retain my sanity under circumstances that were totally alien to me, and doing that took a great deal of courage, few brains, and little thought.

So, actually, what I have written about Normandy is more

form than substance.

And it is enough...

30

Of my sixteen man stick, that fateful night, eleven had landed on the Mereret River, myself and four others on the east side. I never saw the following five men again...

The fate of the eleven men who landed on the west side of the Merderet River made no sense at all considering they all cleared the aircraft in a matter of seconds. Yet Seebach and Thompson were the only guys to get together almost immediately after they had landed. Of the five of us that landed on the east side of the river, only Rickard failed to join up with the four of us. Almost the exact same stick had made two night jumps prior to Normandy and had little trouble rolling up. Admittedly, the speed of our aircraft, turbulence from the ground fire, and weather all played a part in the jump pattern and wide dispersal of the first eleven. But the last five of us had some problems, yet landed reasonably close to one another, even if in the marshes.

Of my 16-man stick that fateful night, eleven had landed on the west side of the Merderet River, myself and four others on the east side. I never saw the following five men again:

#1. Lt. Mac Cook. He rejoined the company sometime after June 15th. He was killed in action July 4th.

#3. Pvt. Cal Morrison. Severely wounded. Never returned to the company.

#6. Pfc. Dan Miller. Severely wounded. Never returned to the company.

#7. Pfc. Frank McAvoy. Taken prisoner June 6th.

#11. Cpl. Don Wright. Taken prisoner June 6th.

My group

#12. Pvt. Cliff Cunningham. Medically evacuated on June 16th. Sent home, received medical discharge.

#14. Pvt. Don Yoon. Killed in action July 4th.

15. Sgt. Bob Broderick. Wounded June 13th. Returned to duty after Normandy.

#16. S/Sgt. George Menter. Wounded June 20th. Returned to duty after Normandy.

Other

#8. Pvt Eddie Vaught. Came across Merderet to where we were on the morning of D-Day. Wounded by   rocket fire later that day. Reassigned to Service Company.

#9. Pfc. Gerald Brightsman. Hill 30 defender. Reunited

with us on June 11th. Wounded July 4th. Returned to duty after Normandy. KIA Sept. 18th.

The following were not with my group during my brief stay in Normandy, but they surfaced later:

#2. Cpl. Jim Jackman. Injured June 6th. Evacuated. Reassigned to Service Company after Normandy.

#4. Pfc. Del Seebach. Rejoined the company sometime after June 15th (had been surrounded by Germans.)

#5. Pfc. Harry Thompson. Rejoined the company sometime after 15th. (had been surrounded by Germans.)

#10. Pfc. Al Ferguson. Wounded early on. Evacuated. Returned to duty after Normandy.

#13. Pfc. Pat Rickard. Wounded early on. Returned to duty after Normandy. KIA Sept.18th.

My officers

Lt. Fred Gillespie had been my platoon leader since basic training, and for the next eighteen months, had been the platoon's only officer, even though all other platoons had the regulation two officers. Lt. Cook was with us only from Ireland to Normandy. Gillespie was truly an officer and a gentleman. We were together constantly and shared all the misery and discomforts of infantry life. Just before our take-off for Normandy, I went over to his aircraft and shook hands with Joe Harrold and him. We wished each other the usual "good luck"

BS and then Gillespie said, "I'll see you on the ground, Brod..." I never saw him again. He was killed by machine gun fire during the early hours of D-Day.

Lt. Mac Cook, who joined us in Ireland, was, like Lt. Gillespie, an ROTC graduate, never an enlisted man. The son of a wealthy southerner, he was a wonderful officer. An early paratrooper, he had been seriously injured during a training jump and could have stayed in the States on limited service. He was to die during the fight for Hill 95. Already wounded in the legs, he was propped up against a hedgerow, kidding those around him about all the beer he'd soon be drinking in Nottingham when another burst from an 88 mm sent shrapnel into his chest, killing him instantly.

Epilogue

Some months ago I responded to an inquiry from Father Thuring. My memory isn't a hell of a lot better now than it was then. I don't know about George Menter, but I can't seem to remember too much about those days and what memories I do have grow dimmer with each passing year. Oh, I still stare at the ceiling more often than I like, but always in bits and pieces. Menter and I were together throughout our time in combat, so I hope he will help fill in some of the blanks.

Some time ago, I received a letter from John Blower who quoted a remark attributed to Mark Twain that went something like, "I remember some things in great detail that never happened." That quote may be appropriate for what is to follow.

As far as I am personally concerned, the Normandy Campaign was such a terrible fiasco that I find it impossible to piece together a reasonable sequence of events from the time we jumped until the time I got shot. But I do recall that what was left of the company that assembled on Hill 30 on or about the 11th of June numbered less than one third of our original company. We had no knowledge at that time of the fate of the rest of the guys. During the afternoon of the 12th, we received a resupply of ammunition and rations and that night made the Douve River crossing to attack the town of Beuzeville La Bastille. So I remember D-Day quite clearly, and the 13th of June reasonably well. But the days in between are very vague. We seemed to be constantly engaged in small deadly encounters with the Germans, but nothing very spectacular. Most of the guys were strangers, anyhow. So that's why I say what I do remember is in bits and pieces, thus suspect. And as I was shot during the attack on Bauapte, I missed the tragic battles for Hills 131 and 95. Seebach and Thompson survived those two killing fields and may be able to pinpoint those company guys that died taking those damn hills.

And the mind plays tricks, especially after all this time. An example may suffice. I called Ted Le Free, who happens to live a few miles from me and told him of your request for updated information on those in the company who were killed in action. As a former F Company Battalion S-2, he was with the the guys who fought for Hill 95. As we shared information, he said he was absolutely certain he saw Kellogg killed during the attack. He was somewhat dismayed when I told him Kellogg wasn't even in Normandy, but was later killed in Holland. I guess we can all relate to some variation on that theme...

While George Menter and I survived all the rest of the battles, nothing we encountered subsequent to Normandy came close to the chaos and appalling casualties of that battle, roughly 85%. But, for what it's worth, the following is a reasonable accounting of our Company's KIA's.

NORMANDY

* Capt. Flanders was killed by Spitfires.

* Generally agreed that Lilly, King, Lazarro, and Prieto were killed still in their chutes.

* Lt. Snee was killed trying to cross the Merderet River under intense enemy fire to where we were at La Fiere.

* Billington was killed during the defense of Hill 30.

* Kulwicki, Lokan, Niemic, and Kincaid were all killed during the attack on Baupte. Kulwicki fell just moments after I got hit.

* Lt. Cook, Harrold, Yoon, Kellum, Montgomery, Chipman, Sprinkle, and others during the attacks on Hills 131 and 95.

* Sometime between the 10th and 11th of June, I remember seeing Lockwood and either Fabuz or Piatt, probably both, still lying where they had fallen, which was some obscure place where our guys and the Germans fought. The dead were everywhere. I recognized some of them from the 2nd Battalion, including the adjutant, but some names escape me. Menter and I tried to identify as many of our own guys as possible, but finally gave up. It was bloody awful. The sight and smell of death was

everywhere around us.

* Sadly, there were simply so many: Lt. Gillespie, Bennett, Martin, D.P. Miller, and a couple dozen other "F" Company guys that died fighting among strangers. We will never know the circumstances of their deaths. Normandy was like that...

HOLLAND

* Dennison was killed in the air by anti-aircraft fire, moments after he jumped. We were on final approach to the DZ, our aircraft was on fire and going down. The rest of us barely got out. My chute snapped open and I was in the trees.

* Lt. King, Brightsman, Rickard, Smith, Spivey, Kellogg, and Logan died during the attack on Beek.

* Hernandez died at the bridge over the Maas-Waal Canal. I don't remember who else may have been killed there.

* Apodaca died while on outpost in the Bemmel area.

* I can't recall who was killed on Voxhil. We were under heavy artillery fire for hours and things were absolutely chaotic.

* John George was accidentally shot by Dobransky. We had marched ten miles out of Nijmegen and were just sitting around a big fire. He had survived Normandy and Holland...

BULGE AND GERMANY

Although we fought in the Battle of the Bulge from the 18th of December until relieved two long weary months later somewhere in Germany, those days are really vague. Mostly I remember the bitter cold and the snow. And while we were still trying to recover from that Holland fiasco, we were suddenly thrust into the Bulge, so quickly in that that as a Platoon Sergeant I didn't even have time to get to know the replacements in my own platoon. So I don't remember what happened to many new faces sent to us just out of jump school. I know I lost most of them, one way or another, during the time we were fighting, so that when we were finally pulled out of Germany in February of 1945, what was once F company was not much more than an oversized platoon. By this time only a very few of the original company were still on line:

* Sudnicki and Sedan were killed by artillery fire during the last major attack by the Germans, trying to overrun us at Erria.

* Hiner, while out on patrol near Erria.

* Lt. Goodale, Ward, and Nelson were killed twenty feet from me by a roving German patrol that we stumbled into. I don't know where the hell we were. There wasn't any front line, as such. We were simply a part of a huge mopping up operation struggling in four feet of snow through dense forests. Their deaths were just the luck of the draw. Goodale led his platoon into the woods just ahead of me and walked into the Germans.

In addition to the above KIA's there were four in Normandy and two in Holland killed by our own men, but that's best left alone. Sadly, it just happened.

I noted several names listed on your rosters as having been in F Company that I do not recognize. But that is understandable.

As I said, after Normandy guys came and went with alarming regularity. Except for the few remaining old timers, it was impossible to keep track of everyone.

I can't imagine where the good Father will find serial numbers to match our KIA's. Army personnel files, I'd guess. I only had three based on a partial list of those of us awarded the CIB published after Normandy.

Even after all of these years it is still painful to recall those terrible days. And as memories start flooding in, the sense of profound sadness is overwhelming. In some way, I suppose Menter and I could be considered fortunate to have survived all those battles, but that's not much consolation as that damn war continues to haunt us.

Hope the above is of some assistance to you and Father Thuring. Maybe someday I will return to Europe and walk down a road or two to see if my hands can keep from shaking and visit for a moment or two with some of those wonderful young men I was privileged to soldier with who didn't make it back home.

"Of all the capacities that the years diminish, none leaves a greater void that that of the youthful ability for easy friendships without the questioning and restraints that complicate those of later life. I feel a void even now in looking back upon friends gone those days. Together we had been through months and years of wartime discomforts and misery of infantry life, lived in mud and dust, heat and cold. The Company dominated our time and effort. Then it all came down to those days of battle, and for many of them it all ended and for the rest of us, I believe that what has been since has not been exactly the same."

Author Unknown

508th Parachute Infantry
Regiment
United States Army

This is to Certify That:

Robert James Broderick

has satisfactorily completed the prescribed course in Parachute Packing, Ground Training, and has made the required number of Parachute Jumps from a plane in flight. He is, therefore, rated from this date March 7, 1943 as a qualified Parachutist

Ray E. Lindquist

Colonel, 508th Parachute Infantry
Commanding

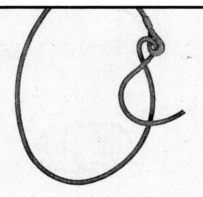

NETHERLANDS CITATION

On October 8, 1945, the 82d Airborne Division became the first non-Dutch unit to be awarded the Militaire Willems Orde, Degree of Knight of the Fourth Class. In addition to having the Division colors decorated, this award entitles all members of the Division who fought in Holland during the period for which the award was made to wear the Orange Lanyard of the Royal Netherlands Army. The 508th Parachute Infantry was part of the 82d Airborne Division at this time. Appropriate quotations from the citation are made below.

I. *Netherlands Decree*

WE, WILHELMINA, by Grace of God, Queen of the Netherlands, Princess of Orange-Nassau, etc., etc., etc.

On the recommendation of Our Ministers of War and for Foreign Affairs, dated October 3, 1945, Secret Nr. Y.22;

In accordance with the provisions of the amended Act of April 30, 1815, Nr.5 (Statute-Book Nr.33);

In view of clause 18 of the regulations of administration and discipline for the Militaire Willems Orde, as laid down in the Royal Decree of June 25, 1815, Nr.10;

Considering the 82d Airborne Division of the United States Army during the airborne operations and the ensuing fighting actions in the central part of the Netherlands in the period from September 17 to October 4, 1944,

II. *Ministerial Decree, Netherlands Government*

MINISTERIAL DECREE OF THE NETHERLANDS MINISTER OF WAR, dated October 8, 1945, Section III, Secret No. X.25.

The Minister of War considering that the outstanding performance of duty of the 82d Airborne Division, United States Army, during the airborne operations and the ensuing fighting actions in the central part of the NETHER-LANDS in the period from September 17 to October 4, 1944, have induced HER MAJESTY THE QUEEN to decorate its Divisional colours with the MILITAIRE WILLEMS ORDE, Degree of Knight of the Fourth Class: considering also that it is desirable for each member of

excelled in performing tasks allotted to it with tact coupled with superior gallantry, self-sacrifice, and loyalty;

Considering also that the actions fought by the aforesaid Division took place in the area of Nijmegen;

HAVE APPROVED AND ORDERED:

1. To decree that the Divisional colours of the 82d Airborne Division of the United States Army shall be decorated with the Militaire Willems Orde, Degree of Knight of the Fourth Class;
2. To authorize the Division to carry in its Divisional colours the name of the town of

NIJMEGEN 1944

Our Ministers of War and for Foreign Affairs are, each for his own part, in charge of the execution of this Decree, copy of which shall be sent to the Chancellor of the Netherlands Orders of Knighthood.

THE HAGUE, October 8, 1945
WILHELMINA

THE MINISTER OF WAR
J. MEIJNEN

THE MINISTER OF FOREIGN AFFAIRS
VAN KLEFFENS

the Division who took part in the aforesaid operations to possess a lasting memento to this glorious struggle;

DECREES: that each member of the personnel of the 82d AIRBORNE DIVISION, UNITED STATES ARMY, who took part in the operations in the area of NIJME-GEN in the period from September 17 to October 4, 1944, is allowed to wear the ORANGE LANYARD, as laid down in article 125g of the Clothing Regulations 1944 of the Royal Netherlands Army.

THE HAGUE, OCTOBER 8, 1945

THE MINISTER OF WAR

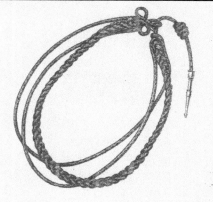

FRENCH CITATIONS

The President of the Provisional Government of the French Republic Cites to the Order of the Army:

508th Parachute Infantry Regiment

A magnificent unit, reputed for the heroism and spirit of sacrifice of its combatants and which has made proof of the greatest military qualities during the battle of Normandy.

It was part of the 82d Airborne Division which, after having occupied roadnets and waterways commanding access to the Cotentin landing places, sacrificed itself on the banks of the Merderet and the Douve, at Saint Sauveur-le-Vicomte and at Etienneville from 6-20 June 1944 in order to restrain at all cost the German reinforcements infinitely superior in strength and fire power, forced them to revert to the defensive and thus permitted the arrival of the bulk of the Allied Forces.

This citation includes the award of the *Croix de Guerre with Palm.*

PARIS, 6 April 1946

Signed: FELIX GOUIN

The President of the Provisional Government of the French Republic Cites the Following Units, being parts of the 82d Airborne Division:

*   *   *   *

508th Parachute Infantry Regiment

*   *   *   *

They are authorized to carry the Fourragère in the colors of the Croix de Guerre, 1939-45.

PARIS, 6 April 1946

Signed: FELIX GOUIN

APPENDIX VII
UNIT CITATIONS

DISTINGUISHED UNIT CITATION

The following is an excerpt from the General Orders conferring upon the 508th Parachute Infantry battle honors for the first three days of fighting in Normandy, France. The award entitles every member of the Regiment to wear the Distinguished Unit Badge.

The 508th Parachute Infantry is cited for outstanding performance of duty in action against the enemy between 6 and 9 June 1944, during the invasion of France. The Regiment landed by parachute shortly after 0200 hours, 6 June 1944. Intense antiaircraft and machine-gun fire was directed against the approaching planes and parachutist drops. Enemy mobile antiairborne landing groups immediately engaged assembled elements of the Regiment and reinforced their opposition with heavily supported reserve units. Elements of the Regiment seized Hill 30, in the wedge between the Merderet and Douve Rivers, and fought vastly superior enemy forces for three days. From this position, they continually threatened German units moving in from the west, as well as the enemy forces opposing the crossing of our troops over the Merderet near La Fiere and Chef-du-Pont. They likewise denied the enemy opportunity to throw reinforcements to the east where they could oppose the beach landings. The troops on Hill 30 finally broke through to join the airborne troops at the bridgehead west of La Fiere on 9 June 1944. They had repelled continuous attacks from infantry, tanks, mortars, and artillery for more than 60 hours without resupply. Other elements of the 508th Parachute Infantry fought courageously in the bitter fighting west of the Merderet River and in winning the bridgeheads across that river at La Fiere and Chef-du-Pont. The Regiment secured its objectives through heroic determination and initiative. Every member performed his duties with exemplary aggressiveness and superior skill. The courage and devotion to duty shown by members of the 508th Parachute Infantry are worthy of emulation and reflect the highest traditions of the Army of the United States.

THE UNITED STATES OF AMERICA

TO ALL WHO SHALL SEE THESE PRESENTS, GREETING: THIS IS TO CERTIFY THAT THE PRESIDENT
OF THE UNITED STATES OF AMERICA AUTHORIZED BY EXECUTIVE ORDER, 24 AUGUST 1962 HAS AWARDED

THE BRONZE STAR MEDAL
(FIRST OAK LEAF CLUSTER)

TO SERGEANT ROBERT J. BRODERICK, UNITED STATES ARMY

FOR Exemplary conduct in ground combat against the armed enemy during
World War II in the European-African-Middle Eastern Theater of
Operations.

GIVEN UNDER MY HAND IN THE CITY OF WASHINGTON

THIS 29th DAY OF March 19 83

_____
The Adjutant General

_____
SECRETARY OF THE ARMY

GENERAL ORDER)
:
NUMBER.....50)

1. Pursuant to the provisions of WD Circular No. 186, 11 May 1944, the following named officers, warrant officers, and enlisted men are awarded the Combat Infantryman's Badge for exemplary conduct in action against the enemy during the NORMANDY, FRANCE campaign, 6 June 1944 to 9 July 1944.

2d Lt. Alsman, Richard C.	O-1307174
1st Lt. Martin, Harold M.	O-1283639
2d Lt. Polette, Lloyd L.	O-1309822
1st Lt. Goodale, Hoyt T.	O-1290034
1st Sgt. Hershman, Kenneth J.	15055517
S/Sgt. Bourne, James	36383801
Pfc. Adamski, Stephen F.	31077339
Pfc. Baughn, Wayne R.	16144642
Sgt. Bell, Glenn	15175336
Pfc. Brightsman, Gerald	39540548
Pfc. Burry, Clarence Y.	14140365
Pfc. Blower, John M.	12198584
Sgt. Broderick, Robert J.	39192574
Pfc. Burns, Dwayne T.	38528118
Pfc. Burrus, Ralph Jr.	35530989
Pvt. Campbell, Jack C.	34729356
Pfc. Carpenter, Joseph R.	11111243
T/4 Chapotan, Edmund D.	39108512
Pfc. Clark, William F.	39029069
T/5 Clevenger, Thomas K.	17154762
Pfc. Colaw, Richard P.	37495050
Pvt. Comeau, Joseph D.	31255974
Pfc. Copeland, Joseph C.	39529132
Pvt. Cunningham, Clifford R.	29319541
Pvt. Dobrucky, John M.	13152004
Pfc. Elash, James A.	35515355
Sgt. Elmore, Thomas Jr.	39109512
Pvt. Ferguson, Albert W.	38403602

7 -

A.P.O. 469, U. S. Army
22   May   1945

GENERAL ORDERS)
            :   E X T R A C T
NUMBER   73)

SECTION

AWARD OF THE SILVER STAR, OAK LEAF CLUSTER...................I
AWARD OF THE SILVER STAR MEDAL..............................II
AWARD OF THE BRONZE STAR MEDAL, OAK LEAF CLUSTER...........III
AWARD OF THE BRONZE STAR MEDAL, FOR MERITORIOUS SERVICE.....IV
AWARD OF THE PURPLE HEART MEDAL..............................V

※※※   ※※※   ※※※

IV --- AWARD OF THE BRONZE STAR MEDAL FOR MERITORIOUS SERVICE:

Under the provisions of AR 600-45, as amended, and pursuant to
authority contained in letter 200.6 (AG) Headquarters XVIII Corps
Airborne, dated 31 August 1944, the following named individuals are
awarded the Bronze Star Medal:

※※※   ※※※   ※※※

ROBERT J. BRODERICK, 39192574, Sergeant, 508th Parachute Infantry. For meritorious service in connection with military operations
against the enemy for the period 6 June 1944 to 17 February 1945
in NORMANDY, HOLLAND, and BELGIUM. Sergeant BRODERICK, Platoon
Sergeant, (then Squad Leader), Company "F", served with his regiment
through all of its campaigns in the European Theater. By his calm
efficiency, and his capacity for anticipating enemy capabilities
Sergeant BRODERICK has been a valuable contribution to the success
of his company's missions. In the attack on ****FRANCE, his skill
in maneuvering his squad resulted in the capture of six 20mm guns.
He - at all times - has demonstrated an exemplary devotion to duty,
and his coolness under fire has inspired his men to great efforts.
Entered military service from SEATTLE, WASHINGTON.

※※※   ※※※   ※※※

By command of Major General GAVIN:

R. H. WIENECKE
Colonel, G.S.C.
Chief of Staff

OFFICIAL: s/ W. E. Stuart
               t/ M. E. STUART
               Lt Col., A.G.D.
               Adjutant General

CERTIFIED A TRUE EXTRACT COPY:

J. F. HUFFMAN , JR., 1st Lt., Inf.

Personnel Officer

October 17, 1988

Hi Bob & George,

The two of you will each receive a copy of this letter explaining
the enclosed KIA-MIA Roster. As you will notice many of the KIA-
MIA lack information as to their final situation. The enclosed
list is an Honor Roll, which will appear on the walls of the
Groesbeek Holland Memorial Building. This effort is being con-
ducted by :

        Father Gerard Thuring
        St. Antoniusweg 2
        Groesbeek - Breedeweg
        The Netherlands

Now, Earl Hickman, Penrose, CO. has the master copy on which he
will transfer any information you can provide. Please show such
information in RED that Earl can easily transcribe the information. Not every member of our Company was fortunate to be sur-
vivors of all four major battles of Europe as you both have experienced. Any information you can offer will certainly be app-
reciated. As for myself I have entered information concerning
13 sitations. In fact two were missing all information request-
ed. Complete any deletions of which you are aware and send to:

        Earl G. Hickman Sr.
        (719)372-3231
        1406 9th Street
        Penrose, CO. 81240

Hop'   ~~th at your best. With the Brodericks
enj   Pacific and the Menters hiding
in   this past summer - I
er   we didn't have
                                                    .fe
Betty   g
on the locat...   naj-
ority request appea...   on-
crete as yet as contact i...   ted
by all of the past and present b...

*[handwritten: Thanks Bob - for updating - you did a great job in
I am glad the KIA-MIA list 2-5-88 believe it or not someone Menter
remembers. difficult one and it's little help but that's life I guess.
Bill]*

P.S. Return the Roster to Earl as soon as p...

                Hope to see you next year,

                        Bill

                        Bill Giegold

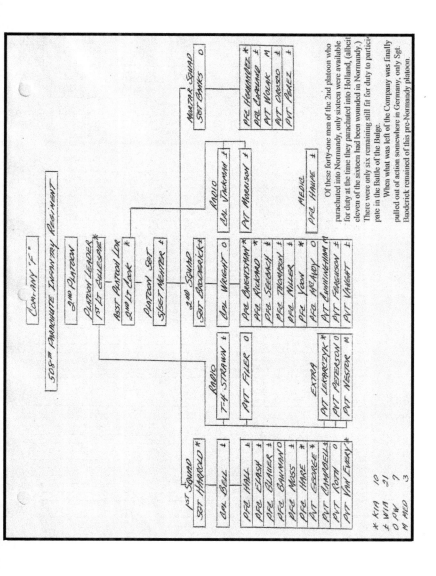

Of these forty-one men of the 2nd platoon who parachuted into Normandy, only sixteen were available for duty at the time they parachuted into Holland, (albeit eleven of the sixteen had been wounded in Normandy.) There were only six remaining still fit for duty to participate in the Battle of the Bulge.

When what was left of the Company was finally pulled out of action somewhere in Germany, only Sgt. Broderick remained of this pre-Normandy platoon

SECRET - (when filled in)

FORM B LOADING MANIFEST (PARACHUTE)

Exercise/Operation **Overlord**

Date **6-5-44**

A/C No. (Tail No.) _____ Chalk No. **32**

PERSONNEL

Drop Order	Army Serial Number	Rank	Full Name	Remarks
1	0-496744	2nd Lt	Cook, Mack G.	
2	39191834	CPL	Jackman, JAMES A.	
3	33653373	PVT	Morrison, CALVIN G.	
4	16073800	PFC	Seebach, DELMAR L.	
5	33674976	PFC	Thompson, HARRY S.	
6	35608804	PVT	Miller, Daniel L.	
7	31136271	PVT	McAvoy, FRANK A.	
8	33526323	PVT	Vaught, Edgar B.	
9	39540448	PFC	Brightsman, GERALD	
10	38403602	PVT	Ferguson, ALBERT W.	
11	39218993	CPL	Wright, DONALD F.	
12	39219541	PVT	Cunningham, CLIFFORD R.	
13	35067850	PVT	Rickard, PATRICK J.	
14	14161395	PFC	Yoon, DONALD	
15	39192574	SGT	Broderick, ROBERT J.	
16	32545237	S/SGT	Menter, GEORGE H.	
17				
18				
19				
20				

MATERIEL

Pack No.	Type	Contents (No.)	Gross Weight	Prcht.	Color/light
#9	A/S	1 - LMG	46		
		4 - BOXES LMG AMMO	74		
#5A		1 - SPARE BARREL	7		
#8A		1 - CAMOUFLAGE NET	10		
		2 - BAGS W/C AP GRENADES	20		
#10	A/S	7 - BOXES LMG AMMO	130		
		30 RDS 60MM AMMO	120		
		2 BLANKETS	8		
	A/S	SPARE LMG - AMMO	300		
	A/S	MINES, AT	300		
Inspection Completed			Signed		

FORM B LOADING MANIFEST (PARACHUTE)

May 31st 1944

Dear Gang:

The rain is beating down in torrents tonight as I lay writing this letter by candle-light. Supping on my hob makes me feel very content and happy tonight.

There are so many things I can think about tonight, but no matter what line I get on my thoughts alway turn to home. That's what keeps all of us going I guess.

Guny and I have been discussing the all-important subject of what there is about rain beating on the old roof that puts everybody in a peaceful and often romantical mood. I hope some day you

will be able to meet Jerry,
for he is quite a fellow.

I was reading in the
papers yesterday about this
"invasion fever" that seems
to have gripped America.
Ball games, races, etc are to
be stopped and prayers offered.
It's a wonderful thought but
for every person who sincerely
offers a prayer there'll be
ten who cuss because of the
interruption of their amuse-
ment. The C.I.O. is a long
way off and not very real.

There is so much to say
tonight I could fill a book
but its getting late now
so guess I'd better close
    Good night gang love
        Bob

Wednesday
February 7, 1945
Belgium

Dear Folks:

Johnny's birthday – guess
that makes him about 26 doesn't
it? Guess the whole gang is
growing up fast now. Doesn't
seem so long ago that we were
all in school and yet it was
six years ago this year since I
graduated from school. Seems
unbelievable.

I'm deadly tired. Last night
I got my first real night's sleep
in a long time and still I really
didn't get any rest – tossed and
turned most of the night. The
events of the last couple of weeks
have been very rough. I consider
myself lucky to have this time
enough to write a letter. Just for
an idea – we figured out to the
best of our ability just how much
sleep (if flopping in snow is sleep) we
got over a certain seven day period.

and it added up to not more than
eight hours. Food was almost non-
existant. It is truely amazing
what you can do if you have to
do it.

In one of the recent letters I
recieved mom remarked how heavy
I was getting. Well I was — guess
I was hitting 175 - 180 lb but not
now. I'd be lucky to hit 150 lbs
with full combat equipment on.

Believe me though — if we are
by all his "men" — never too big once
and for all I can keep right on going.
You'd be surprised at how fiercely
proud we are of being a part of the
82nd. We go so damn fast for the
rest of the Army its funny. As our
S-2 officer said not so long ago "the
U.S. Army can be mighty proud they
are a part of the 82nd.

We joke a lot about the Russian
advance now in that we don't want

to shoot up any Russian patrols. Boy
we hand it to those guys. Who knows—
if we push and keep pushing and they
keep pushing this war may end by
Christmas, though I wouldn't guarantee
it.

I think I told you not so
long ago that Lt. White was hit
and probably would go home. He went
the long way home. Of all the officers
I have ever met or knew he was
probably the finest. He was loved
by all his men — never too big or too
small for anyone. The man just didn't
seem to know fear and when attacking
he was leading. Big, handsome, easy-
going, the most decorated man in the
regiment ———— this war is taking the
best.

I just hope I can get through
the rest now. I'd hate like hell to
get killed at this stage of the game.
Say mom tell the Julia's I got

their package not so long ago and
I certainly did appreciate it. Also
tell them I haven't had any time
during the last three weeks to write
and haven't strength to write any
more today. Perhaps tomorrow or
sometime.

Love
Bob

P.S. Drop John and Tom a line and
tell them I'll write whenever I get
another chance. Also Ann tell Bill.

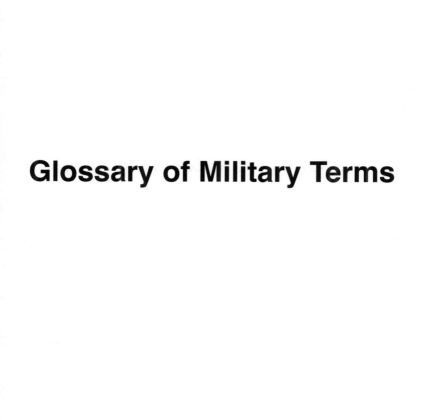

Glossary of Military Terms

1-A – Fit for service.

314 Clipper -- The 314 Clipper was an American long-range flying boat produced by Boeing from 1938 to 1941.

4-F – Unfit for service

40 et 8 – Boxcars used by the French Army marked with "40-8" indicating its capacity to hold 40 men or 8 horses.

57MM – The M1 57MM was a light, easy to maneuver, anti-tank gun on wheels, developed by the British and adopted by the U.S. Army.

A-20 – The Douglas A-20 Havoc was a light-bomber

AWOL – Absent Without Leave

B-17 -- The B-17 Flying Fortress is a four-engine, heavy bomber developed by Boeing in the 1930s for the United States Army Air Corps.

B-24 - A notable departure from other heavy bombers of the era, the B-24 is considered by many to be the greatest bomber of WWII

Bivouac – A temporary encampment where soldiers must remain at the ready for potential attack.

C-47 – The Douglas C-47 Skytrain is a military transport aircraft developed from the civilian Douglas DC-3 airliner.

C-Rations -- Individual ration packaged, pre-cooked foods which could be eaten either hot or cold.

CIB – Combat Infantryman Badge

CQ – Charge of Quarters – A position held by service members in charge of monitoring all traffic in and out of a barracks.

DI – Drill Instructor

DZ – Drop Zone

EM – Emergency Manager

ETO – European Theater of Operations -- The land and sea areas to be invaded or defended

Flak – Germany's main heavy anti-aircraft gun used during WWII

Gammon – Improvised, hand-thrown bomb.

GI – Originally an initialization of standardized type issued or required by the U.S. armed forces turned shorthand for a member or former member of the U.S. armed forces, especially an enlisted soldier.

KIA – Killed in Action

KP – "Kitchen Patrol"

LST – Landing Ship, Tank

M-A-S-H – Mobile Army Surgical Hospital

MP – Military Police

NCO – Non-Commissioned Officer

OD – Olive-Drab

PFC – Private First Class

PX – Post Exchange (A retail store found on U.S. military bases worldwide.)

RAF – Royal Air Force

ROTC – Reserve Officers' Training Corps

Salvo – The simultaneous discharge of artillery or firearms.

Sand Tables – A table bearing a three-dimensional model of a terrain built to scale for study or demonstration of military tactics.

Stick -- The group of paratroopers jumping from an aircraft, at one time, into a drop zone.

Tracers -- illuminated bullets and small caliber artillery shells – usually every fifth round – as an aid for following the trajectory

WAC – Women's Army Corps

Lightning Source UK Ltd.
Milton Keynes UK
UKHW020647160822
407375UK00009B/586